Charting the Major Forex Pairs

Founded in 1807, John Wiley & Sons is the oldest independent publishing company in the United States. With offices in North America, Europe, Australia and Asia, Wiley is globally committed to developing and marketing print and electronic products and services for our customers' professional and personal knowledge and understanding.

The Wiley Trading series features books by traders who have survived the market's ever changing temperament and have prospered—some by reinventing systems, others by getting back to basics. Whether a novice trader, professional or somewhere in-between, these books will provide the advice and strategies needed to prosper today and well into the future.

For a list of available titles, please visit our Web site at www.WileyFinance.com.

Charting the Major Forex Pairs

Focus on Major Currencies

JAMES L. BICKFORD
MICHAEL D. ARCHER

1807
WILEY
2007
BICENTENNIAL

John Wiley & Sons, Inc.

Published by John Wiley & Sons, Inc., Hoboken, New Jersey
Published simultaneously in Canada

Wiley Bicentennial Logo: Richard J. Pacifico

Limit of Liability/Disclaimer of Warranty: While the publisher and author have used their best efforts in preparing this book, they make no representations or warranties with respect to the accuracy or completeness of the contents of this book and specifically disclaim any implied warranties of merchantability or fitness for a particular purpose. No warranty may be created or extended by sales representatives or written sales materials. The advice and strategies contained herein may not be suitable for your situation. You should consult with a professional where appropriate. Neither the publisher nor author shall be liable for any loss of profit or any other commercial damages, including but not limited to special, incidental, consequential, or other damages.

For general information on our other products and services or for technical support, please contact our Customer Care Department within the United States at (800) 762-2974, outside the United States at (317) 572-3993 or fax (317) 572-4002.

Wiley also publishes its books in a variety of electronic formats. Some content that appears in print may not be available in electronic books. For more information about Wiley products, visit our web site at www.wiley.com.

Library of Congress Cataloging-in-Publication Data:

Archer, Michael D. (Michael Duane)
    Charting the major Forex pairs : focus on major currencies / Michael
  Archer, Jim Bickford.
      p.   cm.—(Wiley trading series)
  Includes bibliographical references and index.
  ISBN 978-0-470-12046-0 (pbk.)
    1. Foreign exchange rates—Mathematical models.   2. Foreign exchange market.
  I. Bickford, Jim L.   II. Title.
  HG3852.A78   2007
  332.4'5—dc22

                                                            2006036654

Printed in the United States of America.

10 9 8 7 6 5 4 3 2 1

Contents

Acknowledgment

We wish to thank Paul J. Szeligowski, friend and economic analyst, for his editorial assistance in the preparation of this book. His insightful recommendations and novel ideas proved invaluable in researching the nature of and the occasionally cryptic relationships between the major currency pairs.

About the Authors

Michael D. Archer has been an active commodity futures and Forex trader for more than 30 years. Mike has also worked in various registered advisory capacities, notably as a Commodity Trading Advisor (CTA) and as an investment advisor. He is currently CEO of www.FxPraxis.com, a website specializing in currency trading instruction and money management. His special interest is in complexity theory, especially cellular automata, applied to Forex trading. James L. Bickford is a senior software engineer, technical analyst, and also a very active Forex day trader with an academic background in applied mathematics and statistics. He has numerous books to his credit and recently published *Chart Plotting Algorithms for Technical Analysts*.

The co-authors also collaborated on another best-selling Wiley title, *Getting Started in Currency Trading* (2005).

Introduction

Trading in the foreign exchange currency markets has recently exceeded $2 trillion a day and this figure is expected to double within the next five years. The reason for this astonishing surge in trading popularity is quite simple: no commissions, low transaction costs, easy access to online currency markets, no middlemen, no fixed lot order sizes, high liquidity, low margin with high leverage, and limited regulations. These factors have already attracted the attention of both neophyte traders and veteran speculators in other financial markets.

In this volume, special focus is given to the five most frequently traded Forex currency pairs: the U.S. Dollar, the Euro currency, the British Pound, the Swiss Franc and the Japanese Yen. It is estimated that trading among these five pairs comprises 78 percent of all orders in the spot currency markets.

ABOUT THIS BOOK

This book was written specifically for those currency and futures traders who have a reasonable degree of experience in the foreign exchange markets and who are familiar with the inner trading mechanisms and the risks and rewards intrinsically involved. For novice currency traders, we highly recommend *Getting Started in Currency Trading* by the co-authors of this book (Wiley, 2005) as a comprehensive primer for entering this once exclusive arena of investing.

The authors have intentionally followed the thematic precedent established in their previously published book entitled *The Forex Chartist Companion* (Wiley, 2007). That precedent is to make each technical analysis opus as visual and graphic as possible, replete with numerous charts, tables, and explanatory diagrams. Many of the innovative tools introduced in that work (FCC) are employed here, and the underlying theme is again borne out in this tome: *The most lethal weapons in the successful traders' arsenals are the diversity and creativity of their technical charts.*

HOW THIS BOOK IS ORGANIZED

There are eight major divisions in this book:

Part I: Getting Started

In this section, we expose little known characteristics unique to spot currency data and define the mathematical and statistical tools that facilitate the visual approach to technical analysis.

Part II: Euro Currency

It is only fitting to begin our analysis of major currency pairs with the most heavily traded pair: the EURUSD. A comprehensive history and a detailed account of the Euro's modern evolution are included here. More importantly we supply numerous charts depicting the status of the Euro currency in today's marketplace.

Part III: British Pound

The old adage "The sun never sets on the British Empire" applies to its official currency too. This king of currencies has the highest parity ratio of all the major currencies (1 Pound = 1.70 U.S. Dollars) and is subjected to detailed analysis in this section.

Part IV: Swiss Franc

The Swiss Franc has always held a position of respect and honor in the financial community. Switzerland's political neutrality and banking policies have contributed to its almost mystical attraction. In this section, we reveal its innermost secrets and mathematical properties.

Part V: Japanese Yen

To characterize the Japanese Yen with only one word, it would have to be "resilient." Its decline and recovery history is very impressive. Of all the major currencies, it has the lowest parity ratio (110 Yen = 1 U.S. Dollar). The Yen is heavily influenced by Japanese banking policies and national intervention, the technical results of which are thoroughly examined in this section.

Part VI: Cross Rates

In this section, we examine the six non-USD cross rates: EURGBP, EURCHF, EURJPY, GBPCHF, GBPJPY, and CHFJPY which, fortunately, no longer carry outlandish transaction costs, making them now available to small-cap investors.

Part VII: Comparative Studies

Here we analyze spot currency prices with comparable futures prices and precious metals. We also examine a global synthetic currency called the *Mundo* that we concocted in order to describe the interrelationships between price fluctuations within the five major currencies.

Appendixes

Additional Forex information is provided in this section. After the appendixes, readers will find a list of resources that will help them further their currency trading education.

DISCLAIMER

We wish to emphasize that spot currency trading may not be suited to everyone's disposition. All investors must be keenly aware of the risks involved and of the consequences of ineffective trading habits and/or mismanaged resources. Neither the publisher nor the authors are liable for any losses incurred while trading currencies.

PART I

Getting Started

CHAPTER 1

Understanding
Forex Data

OVERVIEW

Every Forex trade involves the simultaneous buying of one currency and the selling of another currency. These two currencies are always referred to as the *currency pair*. The *base currency* is the first currency in the pair and the second currency in the pair is called the *quote currency*. The *exchange rate* defines how much the base currency is worth in terms of the quote currency.

A common practice in the trade is to describe currency pairs as major currencies, minor currencies or cross rates. Cross rates are those currency pairs in which neither currency is the U.S. Dollar (USD). In major and minor currencies either the base currency or the quote currency is the USD.

Minor currencies are defined as those currency pairs with low trading activity, while the major currencies are those currency pairs with the highest trading volume. Different currency brokers list different pairs as being major or minor. On the average, major currencies carry a slightly lower transaction cost due to their high liquidity. In this book, we arbitrarily define the major pairs as the U.S. Dollar versus the Euro currency, the British Pound, the Swiss Franc, and the Japanese Yen.

A pip is the smallest unit of price that any currency pair can fluctuate. Nearly all currency pairs consist of five significant digits, and most pairs have the decimal point immediately after the leftmost digit; for example, EURUSD is displayed as 1.2329. In this instance, a single pip equals the smallest change in the fourth digit to the right of the decimal point, that is, 0.0001. Therefore, if the quote currency in any pair is the USD, then one pip equals 1/100 of a U.S. cent.

Just as a pip is the smallest price movement along the y-axis, a tick is the smallest unit of time (x-axis) that occurs between two trades. When trading the most active currency pairs during peak trading periods, multiple ticks may and will occur within the

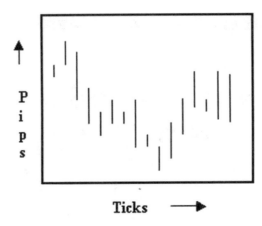

FIGURE 1.1   Pip-Tick Relationship

span of a single second. In fact, over 300 ticks per second are not unusual in the EURUSD during high-activity periods. When trading minor currencies during low-volatility periods, the trader should be aware that a single tick may not occur but every two or three hours. (See Figure 1.1.)

STREAMING DATA

In order to compile an analytical study of this depth, it was necessary to acquire massive amounts of raw historical quotes. To this extent, we wish to express our appreciation to Disk Trading, Ltd. (www.disktrading.com) for its extensive and well-organized archive of historical currency prices (both spot and futures) dating back to the early 1970s.

Forex data can be packaged either as streaming data or as interval data. Streaming data consists of every single price change as it occurs regardless of the time elapsed between ticks. This creates voluminous amounts of data. For example, all the tick quotes for the EURUSD currency pair from January 1, 2005, to December 31, 2005, provide the statistical sample for numerous analyses in this book with a sample size of 7,974,098 prices.

Streaming data uses the following comma-delimited field conventions for tick data:

Date,Time,Close
01/01/2002,0116,0.8896
01/01/2002,0116,0.8895
01/01/2002,0116,0.8897
01/01/2002,0116,0.8893
01/01/2002,0126,0.8902

Data is shipped on compact disks and DVDs since the sheer volume of data is too large to download at current modem speeds. CSV (Comma separated values) files must be unzipped and then read as flat ASCII files.

INTERVAL DATA

Interval data, in contrast, is compiled from the streaming data by coercing the data into the standard open, high, low, and close (OHLC) format for equal-interval time periods. Disk Trading, Ltd., packages this type of data as 1-minute, 5-minute, 10-minute, 30-minute, hourly, and daily data.

Interval data is stored in the following convention (5-minute interval example):

```
Date,Time,O,H,L,C,U,D
4/20/1998,0920,1.0982,1.0982,1.0982,1.0982,2,0
4/20/1998,0925,1.0980,1.0983,1.0980,1.0983,3,1
4/20/1998,0930,1.0985,1.0990,1.0982,1.0989,8,3
4/20/1998,0935,1.0987,1.0993,1.0987,1.0988,2,3
4/20/1998,0940,1.0987,1.0989,1.0983,1.0985,4,3
```

Dates are always expressed using the standard convention MM/DD/YYYY, while the time field uses a four-digit integer to represent the 24-hour convention (i.e., 2030 = 8:30 P.M.).

Due to the lack of centralization, Forex currency data does not have volume and open interest fields as in commodity futures quotes. The last two fields above ("U" and "D") are upticks and downticks. These two fields will be used to calculate two indicators specific to currency trading, the Activity Oscillator and the Direction Oscillator. Activity is calculated as the sum of the upticks and downticks over a specified period. Direction is the difference between upticks and downticks over a specified period.

CHAPTER 2

Tools of the Trade

OVERVIEW

In *The Forex Chartist Companion* (Wiley, 2006), we introduced several innovative charting techniques and some new technical analysis tools. In this chapter we review the ones used in this analysis of the major currency pairs.

It is because of the highly chart-intensive nature of the book that we are compelled to provide very precise definitions of our chart time components to avoid any confusion.

The *time frame* of a chart is the overall duration that the chart spans. On the left side of the chart is the starting date and time and on the right side is the ending date and time. Date and time are represented in the conventional MM/DD/YY HH:MM format. The 24-hour (military) time format is used throughout.

The *time interval* of a chart is the equally spaced time unit into which the time frame is divided. In the case of a vertical OHLC bar chart, the time interval is the width along the x-axis of a single OHLC bar, that is, the amount of time elapsed between the opening quote of the OHLC bar and the closing quote of the same vertical OHLC bar.

ACTIVITY

The concept of activity is employed as a means to evaluate the intrinsic characteristics of a specific currency pair and acts as a surrogate tool for trading volume, a statistic not readily available for spot currencies due to the decentralized nature of Forex markets. (See Figure 2.1.)

Theoretically, activity represents the number of price changes within a given interval of time. Unfortunately, the activity number does not show the size of each order.

$$\text{Activity} = \text{Upticks} + \text{Downticks}$$

FIGURE 2.1 Activity Formula

Nonetheless, this is a case in which any information is better than no information. Thus activity is more representative of trading volatility than actual trading volume.

DIRECTION

For the purpose of this book, we define direction as the difference between the number of upticks and the number of downticks over a specified period of time for a single currency pair. (See Figure 2.2.)

We wish to clarify that there is no direct correlation between our arbitrary definition and that of J. Welles Wilder, the noted trader/author of the 1970s who developed the Average Directional Index (ADX), which uses a Positive Directional Indicator and a Negative Directional Indicator to evaluate the strength of a trend. Further information on Wilder's method can be found in his highly acclaimed book entitled *New Concepts in Technical Trading Systems* (Trend Research, 1978).

ABSOLUTE RANGE

Range—or, more accurately, absolute range—is one of the trader's most important tools for deciphering the hidden personality of an underlying security and is simply the difference between the highest high and the lowest low over a period of time. (See Figure 2.3.)

An increase in range nearly always indicates that a new trend is developing, whereas a decrease in range usually marks either the end of a trend or a reversal in trend.

$$\text{Direction} = \text{Upticks} - \text{Downticks}$$

FIGURE 2.2 Direction Formula

$$\text{Absolute Range} = \text{Highest High} - \text{Lowest Low}$$

FIGURE 2.3 Absolute Range Formula

$$\text{Midrange} = \frac{\text{Highest High} + \text{Lowest Low}}{2}$$

FIGURE 2.4 Midrange Formula

MIDRANGE

Another classical statistic based on the highest high and the lowest low is called the midrange and is the midpoint between the two extremes. (See Figure 2.4.)

RELATIVE RANGE

Whereas the absolute range described earlier is an excellent tool for use in the analysis of the internal characteristics within a single individual security, relative range is used to compare the characteristics of two or more similar securities. (See Figure 2.5.)

The denominator is a critical central point (the midrange in this instance) that converts an individualized statistic into a generalized statistic that is ideal for comparing different sets of similar data. Where absolute range is expressed in terms of pips of the quote currency in the currency pair, relative range is expressed as a percentage and acts as a dimensionless index number. It is this characteristic that permits comparisons between different currency pairs.

A relative range chart differs only slightly from the absolute range chart described earlier in this chapter: The vertical bars in the lower half of the chart are slightly smoothed, and the lower right scale is expressed in percents instead of pips.

Relative range is a measure of relative volatility and can be used to assist the trader in determining which currency pairs to monitor based on the trader's predilection for the ubiquitous risk/reward factor. Trading pairs with high relative ranges increases the risk factor while also increasing the likelihood of greater profits.

A high relative range does not mean that a currency pair is more actively traded than other pairs. Instead, it implies that over time the underlying security prices will travel greater distances from a critical statistical point (in this case, the midrange point).

$$\text{Relative Range} = 100 \times \frac{\text{Absolute Range}}{\text{Midrange}}$$

FIGURE 2.5 Relative Range Formula

$$\text{Absolute Momentum}_n = \text{Abs}(\text{Close}_n - \text{Close}_{n-lag})$$

FIGURE 2.6 Absolute Momentum Formula

ABSOLUTE MOMENTUM

Standard momentum (one close minus a previous close separated by *lag* time units) generates a stream of data consisting of both positive and negative numbers whose mean approaches zero in large samples. To rectify this intrinsic mathematical property, it was necessary to use the absolute value of the momentum data streams. That is, all negative numbers are converted to positive numbers. (See Figure 2.6.)

Thus, when using absolute momentum, we are not concerned about the direction of the processed data since all absolute momentum values are positive. We are, however, very interested in the magnitude of the processed data. Extreme values in an absolute momentum oscillator inform us at what time of day breakouts are most likely to occur, although we do not know which direction they will take. This is, nonetheless, valuable information to traders, particularly for those who subscribe to trend-following techniques.

STANDARD DEVIATION

Of the several methods of calculating the dispersion of a data set from a central point, we prefer to employ the moving standard deviation as the measurement of volatility. Statistically, standard deviation is defined as in Figure 2.7.

$$\text{Variance} = \frac{\Sigma x^2 - \Sigma x^2 / n}{n-1}$$
$$\text{Standard Deviation} = \sqrt{\text{Variance}}$$

FIGURE 2.7 Standard Deviation Formula

where x = the sample elements (prices)
           n = the sample size (number of prices)
    Variance = the sample variance (sum of the deviations squared)

$$\text{Coefficient of Variation} = 100 \times \frac{\text{Standard Deviation}}{\text{Mean}}$$

FIGURE 2.8 Coefficient of Variation Formula

Generally the standard deviation increases as a clear price trend begins emerging in either direction and decreases when lateral congestion originates. A sharp decline in the standard deviation indicates that a price reversal has begun, after which the standard deviation will again increase regardless of the direction of the trend.

COEFFICIENT OF VARIATION

Just as the standard deviation is a measure of absolute dispersion within a single currency pair, the coefficient of variation is a measure of relative dispersion. The coefficient of variation is calculated as in Figure 2.8.

The standard deviation is always expressed in terms of pips in the quote currency, such as dollars, francs, pounds, yen, and so on. The coefficient of variation is expressed as a percentage (or dimensionless index number), which makes it an ideal tool for comparing two or more similar data sets.

Traders should not confuse the coefficient of variation with another statistic called the coefficient of correlation, which measures how closely the estimated values match the raw data in a specified regression model, such as a linear, parabolic, sinusoidal, or logistic regression. The coefficient of variation is analogous to relative range, described earlier.

COMPOSITE CHARTS

Another important analytic tool that we introduced in *The Forex Chartist Companion* is the composite chart, of which we presented two general types: the Time of Day Chart and the Day of Week Chart (defined by their time span, one day or one week respectively).

Composite charts are constructed by averaging one specific statistical category (activity, range, or momentum) over a selected time frame. For example, the daily composite chart in Figure 2.9 illustrates the average range on all Wednesdays between 1/1/2005 and 4/14/2006.

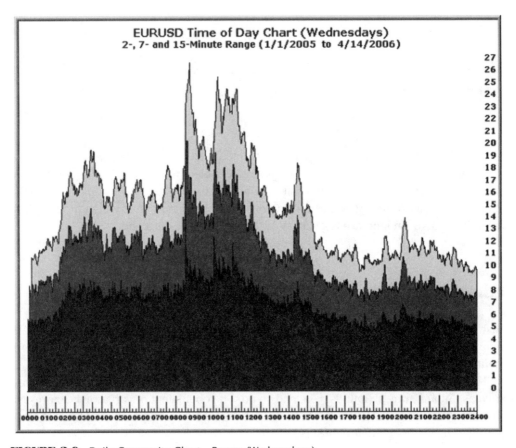

FIGURE 2.9 Daily Composite Chart—Range (Wednesdays)

In a similar manner, the weekly composite chart can be constructed by concatenating the daily charts. In Figure 2.10, the average weekly activity between 1/1/2005 and 4/14/2006 is examined.

Composite charts are designed to assist traders in scheduling their primary trading sessions. In accordance with our time definitions described at the beginning of this chapter, the *time frame* in this chart is Sunday 00:00 through Friday 23:59, or six days. The *time interval* is measured in one- and two-hour increments.

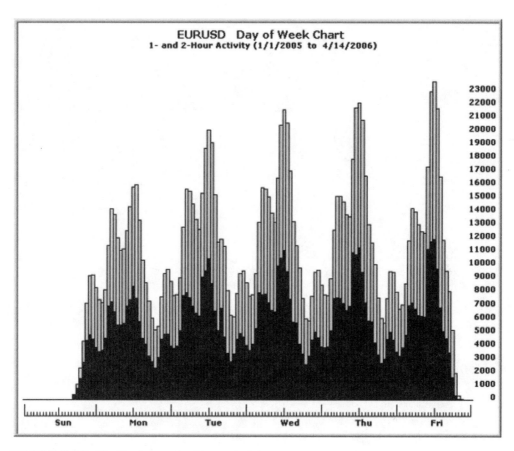

FIGURE 2.10 Weekly Composite Chart—Activity

PART II

Euro Currency

CHAPTER 3

History of the Euro Currency

WHY TRADE THE EURO CURRENCY?

The EURUSD is the most actively traded of all pairs available on the Foreign Exchange markets globally. This fact alone ensures both volatility (that is, prices will fluctuate with sufficient standard deviation to make trading profitable) and liquidity (the ability to enter and exit the market quickly at a specified price).

HISTORICAL PERSPECTIVE

On January 1, 1999, 11 of the countries in the European Economic and Monetary Union (EMU) decided to give up their own currencies and adopt the new Euro (EUR) currency: Austria, Belgium, Finland, France, Germany, Ireland, Italy, Luxembourg, the Netherlands, Portugal, and Spain. Greece followed on January 1, 2001. The Vatican City also participated in the changeover. This changeover is now complete.

It is worth noting that any place that previously used one or more of the currencies listed below has now also adopted the Euro. This applies to the Principality of Andorra, the Principality of Monaco, and the Republic of San Marino. This of course applies automatically to any territories, departments, possessions, or collectivities of Euro-zone countries, such as the Azores, Balearic Islands, the Canary Islands, Europa Island, French Guiana, Guadeloupe, Juan de Nova, the Madeira Islands, Martinique, Mayotte, Reunion, Saint-Martin, Saint Pierre, and Miquelon, to name just a few.

Euro bank notes and coins began circulating in the above countries on January 1, 2002. At that time, all transactions in those countries were valued in Euro, and the "old" notes and coins of these countries were gradually withdrawn from circulation. (See Table 3.1.)

TABLE 3.1 EMU Member Legacy Currencies

ISO	Country	Currency	Conversion to Euro	Conversion from Euro
ATS	Austria	Schilling	ATS / 13.7603 = EUR	EUR × 13.7603 = ATS
BEF	Belgium	Franc	BEF / 40.3399 = EUR	EUR × 40.3399 = BEF
DEM	Germany	Mark	DEM / 1.95583 = EUR	EUR × 1.95583 = DEM
ESP	Spain	Peseta	ESP / 166.386 = EUR	EUR × 166.386 = ESP
FIM	Finland	Markka	FIM / 5.94573 = EUR	EUR × 5.94573 = FIM
FRF	France	Franc	FRF / 6.55957 = EUR	EUR × 6.55957 = FRF
GRD	Greece	Drachma	GRD / 340.750 = EUR	EUR × 340.750 = GRD
IEP	Ireland	Punt	IEP / 0.787564 = EUR	EUR × 0.787564 = IEP
ITL	Italy	Lira	ITL / 1936.27 = EUR	EUR × 1936.27 = ITL
LUF	Luxembourg	Franc	LUF / 40.3399 = EUR	EUR × 40.3399 = LUF
NLG	Netherlands	Guilder	NLG / 2.20371 = EUR	EUR × 2.20371 = NLG
PTE	Portugal	Escudo	PTE / 200.482 = EUR	EUR × 200.482 = PTE
VAL	Vatican City	Lira	VAL / 1936.27 = EUR	EUR × 1936.27 = VAL

ISO stands for the International Standards Organization. Most outgoing pre-Euro currencies will still be physically convertible at special locations for a period of several years. For details, refer to the official Euro site (www.euro.gov.uk).

Also note that the Euro is not just the same thing as the former European Currency Unit (or ECU), which used to be listed as XEU. The ECU was a theoretical basket of currencies rather than a currency in and of itself, and no ECU bank notes or coins ever existed. At any rate, the ECU has been replaced by the Euro, which is a *bona fide* currency.

A note about spelling and capitalization: the official spelling of the EUR currency unit in the English language is "euro," with a lower case "e." However, the overwhelmingly prevailing industry practice is to spell it "Euro," with a capital "E." Since other currency names are capitalized in general use, doing so helps differentiate the noun "Euro," meaning EUR currency, from the more general adjective "euro," meaning anything even remotely having to do with Europe.

BANKNOTES AND COINS

On January 1, 2002, the euro coins came into circulation. The eight denominations of coins vary in size, color, and thickness according to their values, which are 1, 2, 5, 10, 20, and 50 cent, or EUR 1 and EUR 2. One euro is divided into 100 cents.

One side of each coin features one of three designs common to all 12 euro area countries; these designs show different maps of Europe surrounded by the 12 stars of the European Union. The reverse side of each coin shows individual designs relating to the member state where the coin originates, surrounded by 12 stars. Euro coins can be used anywhere in the euro area, regardless of their national sides. Milled edges have been introduced to make it easier, especially for those with impaired sight, to recognize different values. Sophisticated bi-metal technology has been incorporated into the EUR 1 and EUR 2 coins which, together with lettering around the edge of the EUR 2 coin, prevents counterfeiting.

Also on January 1, 2002, the euro banknotes were put into circulation with the following stipulations: There are seven new banknotes; they have the same design throughout Europe; each banknote has a different color and different size; the EUR 5 is the smallest banknote and the EUR 500 the biggest. The banknotes that circulate in denominations of EUR 5, 10, 20, 50, 100, 200, and 500 have pictures of windows, arches, gateways, and bridges on them as well as a map of Europe and the European flag.

14.89 billion euro banknotes have been produced; 10 billion were needed to replace the national banknotes in circulation and nearly 5 billion are to be held in reserve. See Figures 3.1 through 3.5.

FIGURE 3.1 500 Euro Banknote Front and Back

Denomination:	EUR 500
Size:	160×82 mm
Color:	Purple
Architectural period:	Modern 20th century architecture

FIGURE 3.2   200 Euro Banknote Front and Back

Denomination: EUR 200
Size: 153×82 mm
Color: Yellow-brown
Architectural period: Iron and glass architecture

FIGURE 3.3   100 Euro Banknote Front and Back

Denomination:	EUR 100
Size:	147×82 mm
Color:	Green
Architectural period:	Baroque and rococo

FIGURE 3.4   2 Euro Coin Obverse and Reverse

Denomination: EUR 2
Diameter: 25.75 mm
Thickness: 2.20 mm
Weight: 8.50 g
Composition: Outer part: copper-nickel; inner part: three layers: nickel
                       brass, nickel, nickel brass

FIGURE 3.5   1 Euro Coin Observe and Reverse

Denomination: EUR 1
Diameter: 23.25 mm
Thickness: 2.33 mm
Weight: 7.50 g
Composition: Outer part: nickel brass; inner part: three layers: copper-
                       nickel, nickel, copper-nickel

Visit http://www.euro.ecb.int/en/section/testnotes.nd100.html for additional details.

EURO CURRENCY VERSUS EURO DOLLAR

The Euro currency contract is a futures contract of the Euro, the currency in circulation in EMU member nations. The contract size is 125,000 Euros, the minimum fluctuation is $ 0.0001, one point equals $12.50, and contract duration is six months with delivery months in March, June, September, and December.

The Euro dollar futures contract is a time deposit having a principal value of $1,000,000 with a 3-month maturity and is categorized at the exchange as an interest rate rather than a currency. It is based upon the number of U.S. dollars deposited in European banks. Trading contracts occur in each calendar month and each point equals $25.00.

CHAPTER 4

Annual Charts

OHLC AND ACTIVITY CHARTS

In this chapter, we examine historical charts for the years 2000 through 2005 using daily interval data. In the lower portion of each chart, activity is expressed in terms of ticks of the currency pair. See Figures 4.1 through 4.7.

FIGURE 4.1   EURUSD OHLC and Activity 2000

EURUSD Properties 2000

Open	0.9423
High	0.9594
Low	0.8349
Close	0.8901
Midrange	0.8972
Absolute Range	0.1245
Relative Range	13.8773
Arithmetic Mean	0.8960
Standard Deviation	0.0261
Coefficient of Variation	2.9100

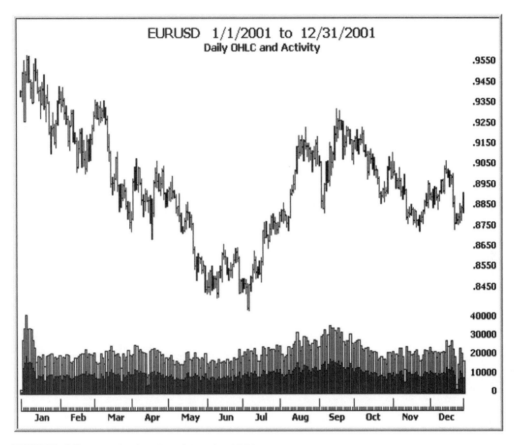

FIGURE 4.2 EURUSD OHLC and Activity 2001

EURUSD Properties 2001

Open	1.0088
High	1.0414
Low	0.8229
Close	0.9423
Midrange	0.9322
Absolute Range	0.2185
Relative Range	23.4404
Arithmetic Mean	0.9238
Standard Deviation	0.0502
Coefficient of Variation	5.4367

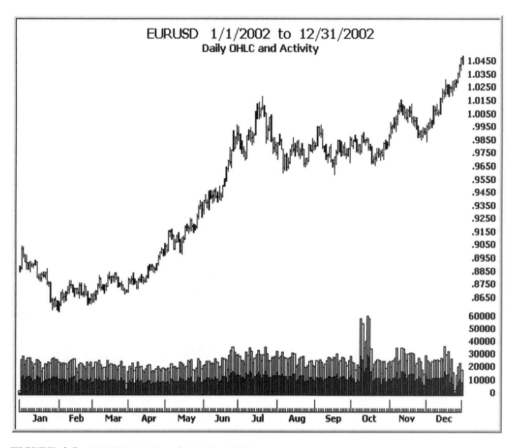

FIGURE 4.3 EURUSD OHLC and Activity 2002

EURUSD Properties 2002

Open	0.8901
High	1.0512
Low	0.8562
Close	1.0494
Midrange	0.9537
Absolute Range	0.1950
Relative Range	20.4467
Arithmetic Mean	0.9462
Standard Deviation	0.0537
Coefficient of Variation	5.6733

FIGURE 4.4 EURUSD OHLC and Activity 2003

EURUSD Properties 2003

Open	1.0494
High	1.2647
Low	1.0331
Close	1.2592
Midrange	1.1489
Absolute Range	0.2316
Relative Range	20.1584
Arithmetic Mean	1.1324
Standard Deviation	0.0509
Coefficient of Variation	4.4907

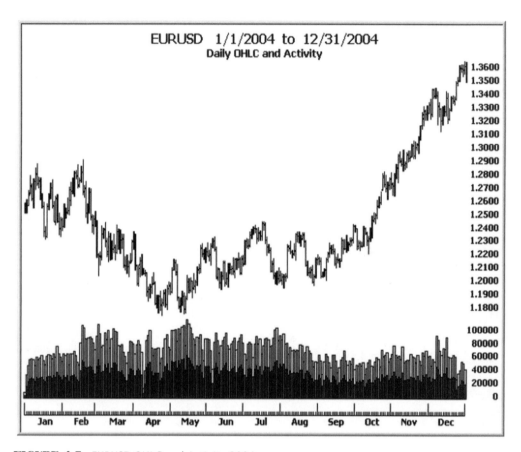

FIGURE 4.5 EURUSD OHLC and Activity 2004

EURUSD Properties 2004

Open	1.2590
High	1.3667
Low	1.1760
Close	1.3553
Midrange	1.2714
Absolute Range	0.1907
Relative Range	14.9998
Arithmetic Mean	1.2440
Standard Deviation	0.0430
Coefficient of Variation	3.4560

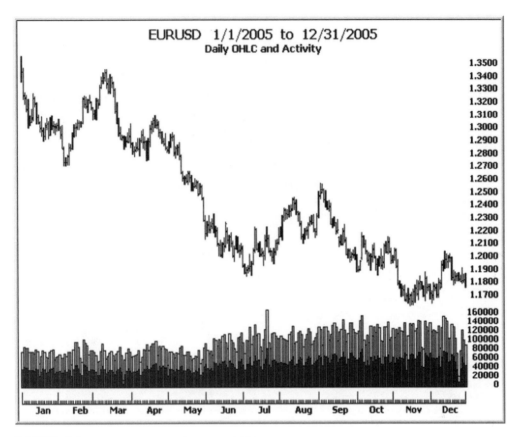

FIGURE 4.6 EURUSD OHLC and Activity 2005

EURUSD Properties 2005

Open	1.3553
High	1.3580
Low	1.1638
Close	1.1849
Midrange	1.2609
Absolute Range	0.1942
Relative Range	15.4017
Arithmetic Mean	1.2442
Standard Deviation	0.0503
Coefficient of Variation	4.0398

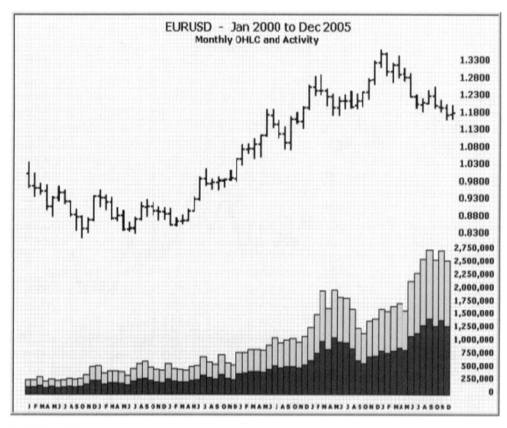

FIGURE 4.7   EURUSD OHLC and Activity 2000–2005

STATISTICS

EURUSD Properties 2000–2005

Year	High	Low	Mean	Rel Range	Coef Var
2000	0.9594	0.8349	0.8960	13.8773	2.9100
2001	1.0414	0.8229	0.9238	23.4404	5.4367
2002	1.0512	0.8562	0.9462	20.4467	5.6733
2003	1.2647	1.0331	1.1324	20.1584	4.4907
2004	1.3667	1.1760	1.2440	14.9998	3.4560
2005	1.3580	1.1638	1.2442	15.4017	4.0398
Avg	1.3667	0.8229	1.0645	14.5723	3.9036

Monthly Charts

OHLC AND ACTIVITY CHARTS

In the current chapter, we examine recent market behavior in the EURUSD currency pair for the months January through March 2006 using daily interval data. See Figures 5.1 through 5.3.

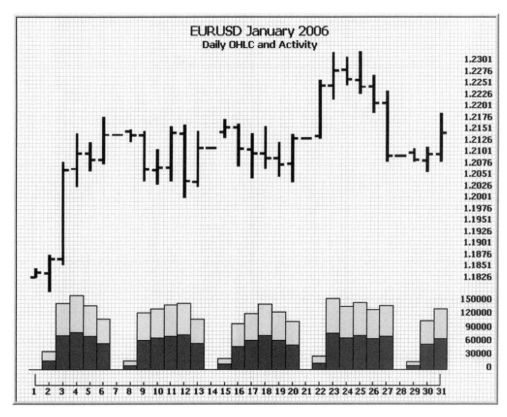

FIGURE 5.1   EURUSD OHLC and Activity January 2006

EURUSD Properties January 2006

Open	1.1833
High	1.2324
Low	1.1801
Close	1.2148
Midrange	0.2063
Absolute Range	0.0523
Relative Range	4.3358
Arithmetic Mean	1.2115
Standard Deviation	0.0092
Coefficient of Variation	0.7586

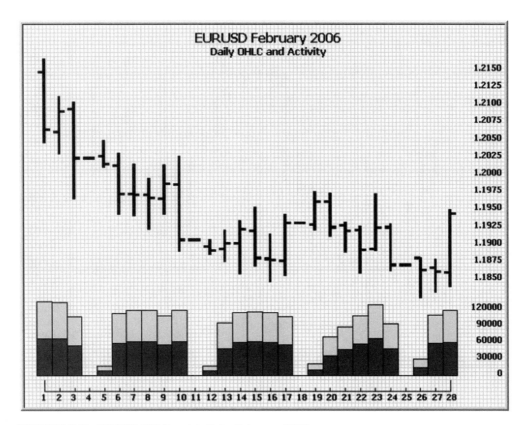

FIGURE 5.2   EURUSD OHLC and Activity February 2006

EURUSD Properties February 2006

Open	1.2148
High	1.2167
Low	1.1825
Close	1.1946
Midrange	1.1996
Absolute Range	0.0342
Relative Range	2.8510
Arithmetic Mean	1.1941
Standard Deviation	0.0062
Coefficient of Variation	0.5153

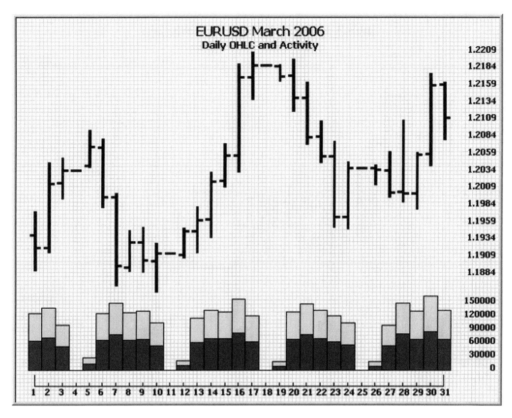

FIGURE 5.3   EURUSD OHLC and Activity March 2006

EURUSD Properties March 2006

Open	1.1942
High	1.2209
Low	1.1859
Close	1.2114
Midrange	1.2034
Absolute Range	0.0350
Relative Range	2.9084
Arithmetic Mean	1.2035
Standard Deviation	0.0088
Coefficient of Variation	0.7332

STATISTICS

EURUSD Properties Jan–Mar 2006

Month	High	Low	Mean	Rel Range	Coef Var
Jan	1.2324	1.1801	1.2115	4.3358	0.7586
Feb	1.2167	1.1825	1.1941	2.8510	0.5153
Mar	1.2209	1.1859	1.2035	2.9084	0.7332
Avg	1.2233	1.1828	1.2030	3.3651	0.6690

A quick survey of the list above indicates that all values fall within expected boundaries. The average daily range during the overall time frame (1/1/2006 through 3/31/2006) was 78 pips.

CHAPTER 6

Composite Charts

DAILY COMPOSITE CHARTS

Refer to Chapter 2, Tools of the Trade, for a detailed description of both daily and weekly composite charts

The time frame in the following charts (Figures 6.1 through 6.9) spans 1/1/2005 through 4/14/2006. Daily composite activity charts are calculated by averaging the sum of the upticks and downticks over that period using one-minute time intervals. Their purpose is to assist traders in determining when to schedule online trading sessions based upon traders' predilection to the nebulous risk/reward factor and the volatility of the targeted currency pair.

The vertical numeric scale on the right of each chart is activity expressed in total number of ticks (upticks plus downticks) during each time interval. The bottom band (the darkest) represents the activity for the current one-minute interval. The central band plus the lower band represents 3-minute activity. The sum of the all three bands represents the 5-minute activity.

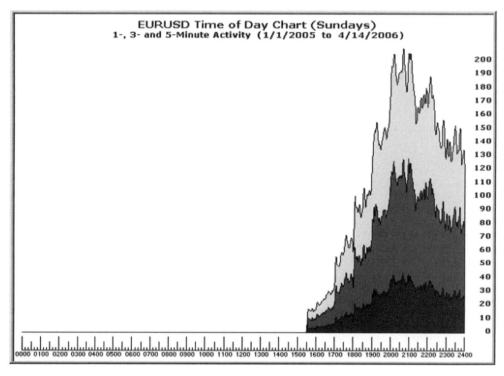

FIGURE 6.1 Sunday Composite Activity Chart

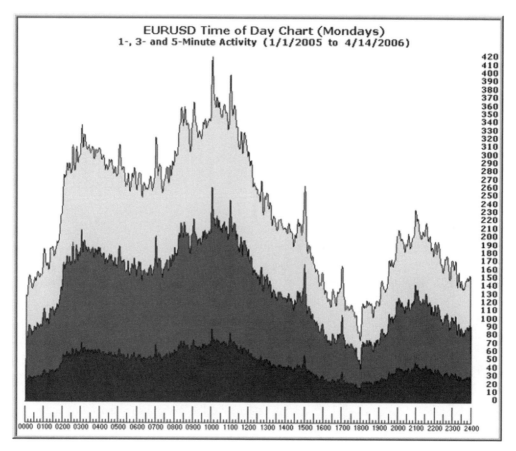

FIGURE 6.2 Monday Composite Activity Chart

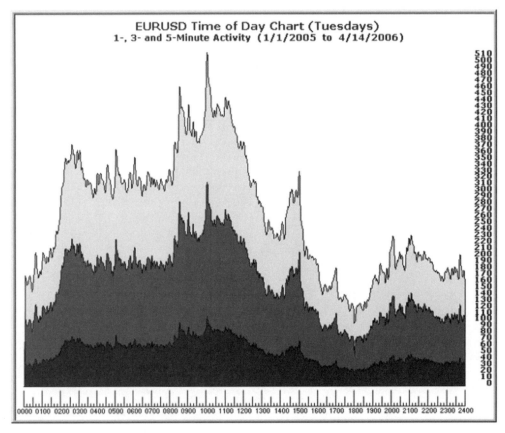

FIGURE 6.3 Tuesday Composite Activity Chart

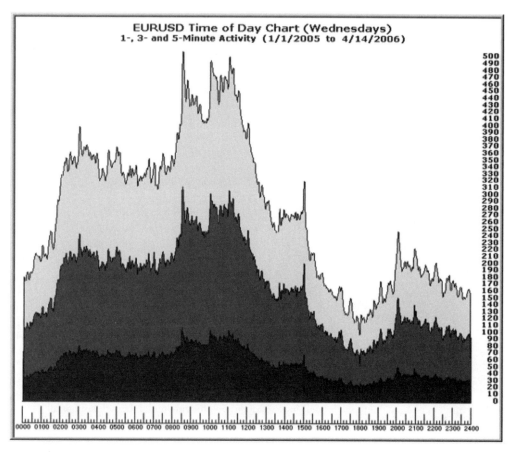

FIGURE 6.4 Wednesday Composite Activity Chart

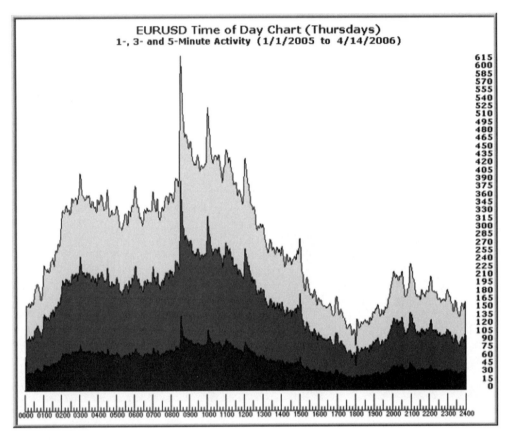

FIGURE 6.5 Thursday Composite Activity Chart

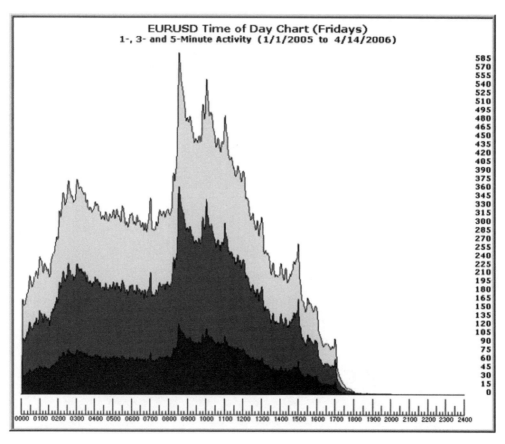

FIGURE 6.6 Friday Composite Activity Chart

A close inspection of the composite charts above reveals that each daily chart is unique. This can be primarily attributed to intervention and to the fact that various regulatory agencies schedule their news releases on different days of the week, and at any time between 8:30 A.M. ET and 4:00 P.M. ET (usually). Without invention, these charts would most likely exhibit a smoother, less "spikey" behavior.

WEEKLY COMPOSITE CHARTS

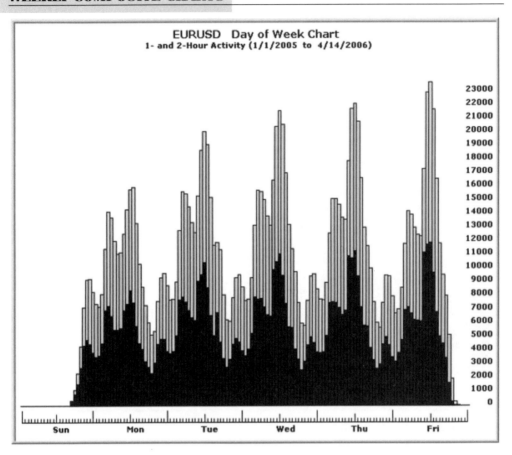

FIGURE 6.7 Weekly Activity Composite Chart

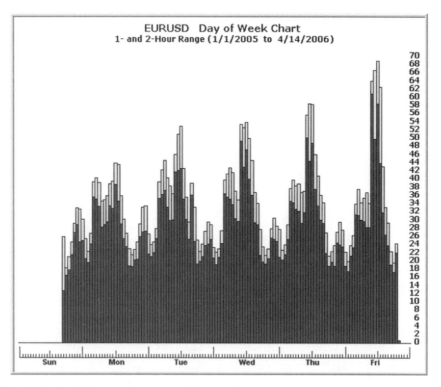

FIGURE 6.8 Weekly Range Composite Chart

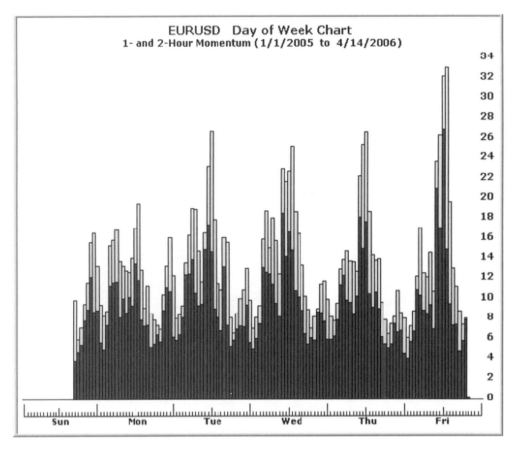

FIGURE 6.9   Weekly Momentum Composite Chart

CAVEAT

Traders should be aware that starting around 3:30 P.M. Eastern Time, many currency brokers begin gradually increasing their transaction costs. One NY broker raises the EURUSD transaction cost from its standard 3 pips to 5 pips. Shortly after 4:00 P.M., this is again incremented to 7 pips then 10 pips by 4:30 P.M. Unless traders intend to stay in an open position over the weekend and risk rollover charges, they should liquidate all trades prior to 3:00 P.M. Friday Eastern Time. It is possible, for whatever reason, to trade over the weekend, but the high transaction costs and lack of volatility usually defeat the prospect of any profitability.

   Additionally, traders should also be aware of another phenomenon which, though it occurs very infrequently, can have a very damaging effect on placing orders. The transaction cost may spike wildly without warning and for no apparent reason. Currency brokers protect themselves whenever the electronic order book becomes lopsided. This book is a list of the incoming trades at the lowest level. Normally, buy orders must be offset with corresponding sell orders of the same quantity, thus maintaining a state of equilibrium (in futures contracts, this equilibrium is rigidly enforced; a long always has a corresponding short). If the number of incoming buy orders far exceeds the number of incoming sell orders (or vice versa), the broker may increase the bid-ask spread to ensure liquidity and to avoid brokerage house losses.

PART III

British Pound

CHAPTER 7

History of the Pound

WHY TRADE THE BRITISH POUND?

Aside from being one of the most actively traded currency pairs, the British Pound holds a position of being the king of currencies in the international arena. Its stability and status as legal tender globally during the period of the British Empire contribute to its appeal.

HISTORICAL PERSPECTIVE

As a unit of currency, the term *pound* originated from the value of a troy pound of high purity silver known as sterling silver. The sterling was originally a name for a silver penny of 1/240 pound. Originally a silver penny had the purchasing power of slightly less than a modern pound. In modern times the pound has replaced the penny as the basic unit of currency as inflation has steadily eroded the value of the currency.

The pound sterling, established in 1560 by Elizabeth I, brought order to the financial chaos of Tudor England that had been caused by the "Great Debasement" of the coinage, which brought on a debilitating inflation during the years 1543–1551. By 1551, the silver content of a penny had dropped to one part in three. The coinage had become a mere fiduciary currency (as modern coins are), and the exchange rate on the European continent deteriorated accordingly. All the coins in circulation were called in for reminting at the higher standard, and paid for at discounted rates.

The pound sterling maintained its intrinsic value uniquely among European currencies, even after the United Kingdom officially adopted the gold standard, until after World War I; it weathered financial crises in 1621, in 1694–1696, and again in 1774 and 1797. Not even the violent disorders of the Civil War devalued the pound sterling in European money markets. England's easy credit, security of contracts, and rise to financial superiority during the 18th century all contributed to the fact that the pound was never devalued over the centuries. The pound sterling has been the money of account of the Bank of England from its inception in 1694.

THE GOLD STANDARD

Sterling unofficially moved to the gold standard from silver due to an overvaluation of gold in England that drew gold from abroad and caused a steady export of silver coin, in spite of a reevaluation of gold in 1717 by Sir Isaac Newton, Master of the Royal Mint. The *de facto* gold standard continued until its official adoption following the end of the Napoleonic Wars in 1816. This lasted until the United Kingdom abandoned the standard after World War I in 1919. During this period, the pound was generally valued at around U.S. $4.90.

In an attempt to resume stability, a variation on the gold standard was reintroduced in 1926, under which the currency was pegged to the gold price at pre-war levels, although people were only able to exchange their currency for gold bullion, rather than for coins. This was abandoned on September 21, 1931, during the Great Depression, and the pound was devalued by 20 percent.

In common with all other world currencies, the pound no longer has any link to precious metals. The U.S. dollar was the last to leave gold, in 1971. The pound was made fully convertible in 1946 as a condition for receiving a U.S. loan of $3.75 billion in the aftermath of World War II. At this time the pound sterling was used as the currency of the British Empire. As the Empire became the Commonwealth of Nations, dominions introduced their own currencies (such as the Australian pound). Visit http://en.wikipedia.org/ for further details.

The post-World War II GBPUSD exchange rates are shown in Figure 7.1:

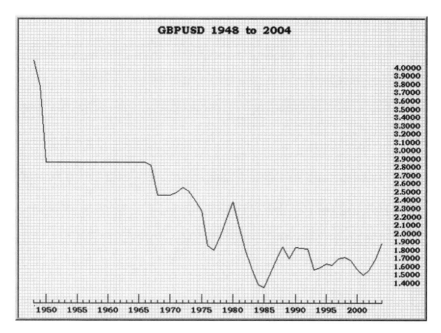

FIGURE 7.1 GBPUSD Annual Closes 1948 to 2004

GBPUSD 1948 to 2004

Year	GBPUSD	Year	GBPUSD	Year	GBPUSD
1948	4.0300	1967	2.7616	1986	1.4659
1949	3.7225	1968	2.4000	1987	1.6342
1950	2.8000	1969	2.4000	1988	1.7788
1951	2.8000	1970	2.4000	1989	1.6362
1952	2.8000	1971	2.4336	1990	1.7756
1953	2.8000	1972	2.4976	1991	1.7636
1954	2.8000	1973	2.4500	1992	1.7551
1955	2.8000	1974	2.3378	1993	1.4998
1956	2.8000	1975	2.2122	1994	1.5304
1957	2.8000	1976	1.7969	1995	1.5781
1958	2.8000	1977	1.7444	1996	1.5602
1959	2.8000	1978	1.9175	1997	1.6371
1960	2.8000	1979	2.1178	1998	1.6561
1961	2.8000	1980	2.3240	1999	1.6180
1962	2.8000	1981	2.0095	2000	1.5130
1963	2.8000	1982	1.7469	2001	1.4396
1964	2.8000	1983	1.5158	2002	1.4987
1965	2.8000	1984	1.3301	2003	1.6327
1966	2.8000	1985	1.2833	2004	1.8309

BANKNOTES AND COINS

As of July 2005, the Bank of England circulates the following banknotes, known as Series E:

- 5-pound note depicting Elizabeth Fry, showing a meeting of people possibly discussing prisoners' rights.
- 10-pound note depicting Charles Darwin, a hummingbird, and the HMS Beagle. (See Figure 7.2.)
- 20-pound note depicting Sir Edward Elgar, with a view of the west face of Worcester Cathedral.
- 50-pound note depicting Sir John Houblon, with a view of his house in Threadneedle Street.

FIGURE 7.2   Ten-Pound Banknote

Currently there are eight British coins in circulation. (See Figures 7.3 and 7.4.)

FIGURE 7.3   One Penny, Two Pence, Five Pence, and Ten Pence

FIGURE 7.4   Twenty Pence, Fifty Pence, One Pound, Two Pound

CHAPTER 8

Annual Charts

OHLC AND ACTIVITY CHARTS

In this chapter, we examine GBPUSD historical charts for the years 2000 through 2005 using daily interval data. In the lower portion of each chart, activity is expressed in terms of ticks (the sum of upticks and downticks). (See Figures 8.1 through 8.7.)

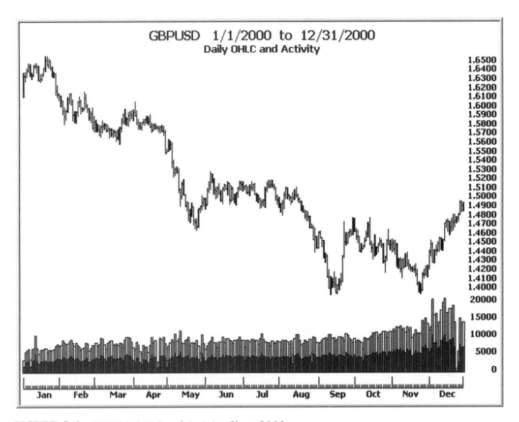

FIGURE 8.1   GBPUSD OHLC and Activity Chart 2000

GBPUSD Properties 2000

Open	1.6147
High	1.6579
Low	1.3953
Close	1.4929
Midrange	1.5266
Absolute Range	0.2626
Relative Range	17.2016
Arithmetic Mean	1.5160
Standard Deviation	0.0681
Coefficient of Variation	4.4941

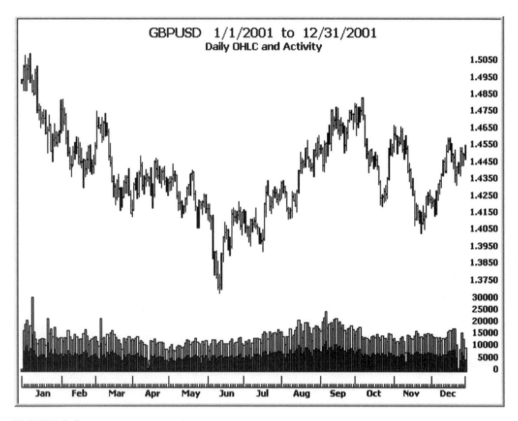

FIGURE 8.2 GBPUSD OHLC and Activity Chart 2001

GBPUSD Properties 2001

Open	1.4929
High	1.5104
Low	1.3685
Close	1.4546
Midrange	1.4395
Absolute Range	0.1419
Relative Range	9.8579
Arithmetic Mean	1.4407
Standard Deviation	0.0237
Coefficient of Variation	1.6444

FIGURE 8.3   GBPUSD OHLC and Activity Chart 2002

GBPUSD Properties 2002

Open	1.4546
High	1.6142
Low	1.4044
Close	1.6098
Midrange	1.5093
Absolute Range	0.2098
Relative Range	13.9005
Arithmetic Mean	1.5038
Standard Deviation	0.0627
Coefficient of Variation	4.1683

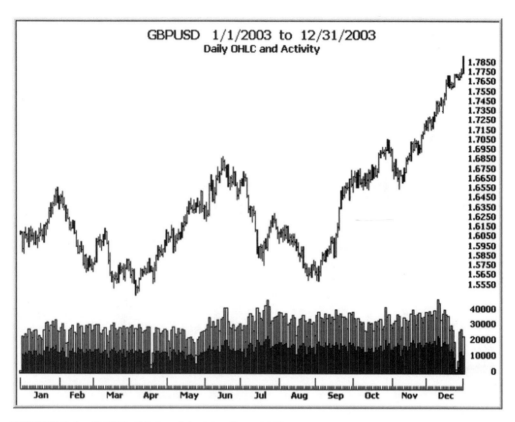

FIGURE 8.4   GBPUSD OHLC and Activity Chart 2003

GBPUSD Properties 2003

Open	1.6098
High	1.7942
Low	1.5462
Close	1.7855
Midrange	1.6702
Absolute Range	0.2480
Relative Range	14.8485
Arithmetic Mean	1.6356
Standard Deviation	0.0536
Coefficient of Variation	3.2764

 BRITISH POUND

FIGURE 8.5 GBPUSD OHLC and Activity Chart 2004

GBPUSD Properties 2004

Open	1.7834
High	1.9550
Low	1.7482
Close	1.9190
Midrange	1.8516
Absolute Range	0.2068
Relative Range	11.1687
Arithmetic Mean	1.8332
Standard Deviation	0.0423
Coefficient of Variation	2.3052

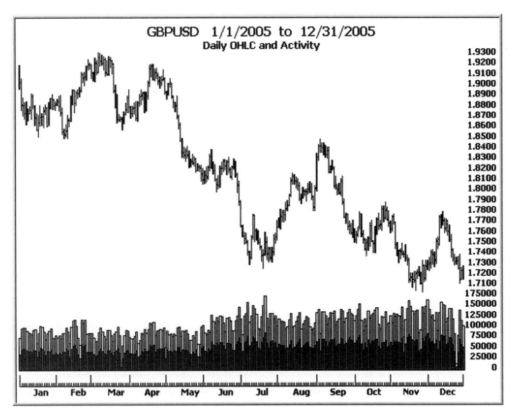

FIGURE 8.6 GBPUSD OHLC and Activity Chart 2005

GBPUSD Properties 2005

Open	1.9183
High	1.9325
Low	1.7047
Close	1.7232
Midrange	1.8186
Absolute Range	0.2278
Relative Range	12.5261
Arithmetic Mean	1.8194
Standard Deviation	0.0626
Coefficient of Variation	3.4433

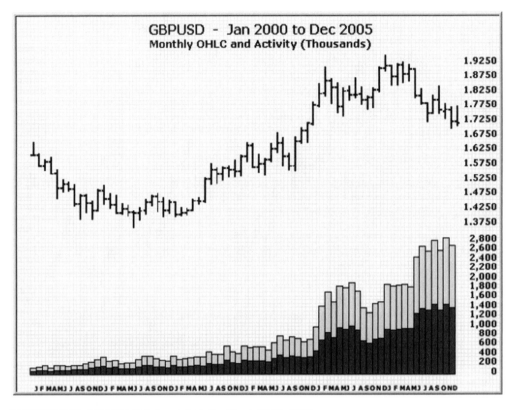

FIGURE 8.7 GBPUSD OHLC and Activity Chart 2000–2005

STATISTICS

The annual data above can be summarized as in the list below.

GBPUSD Properties 2000–2005

Year	High	Low	Mean	Rel Range	Coef Var
2000	1.6579	1.3953	1.5160	17.2016	4.4941
2001	1.5104	1.3685	1.4407	9.8579	1.6444
2002	1.6142	1.4044	1.5038	13.9005	4.1683
2003	1.7942	1.5462	1.6356	14.8485	3.2764
2004	1.9550	1.7482	1.8332	11.1687	2.3052
2005	1.9325	1.7047	1.8194	12.5261	3.4433

A quick survey of the list above indicates that all values fall again within expected boundaries. The average annual range during the overall time frame (1/1/2000 through 3/31/2006) was 2,162 pips.

CHAPTER 9

Monthly Charts

OHLC AND ACTIVITY CHARTS

In the current chapter, we examine recent market behavior in the GBPUSD currency pair for the months January through March 2006 using daily interval data. (See Figures 9.1 through 9.3.)

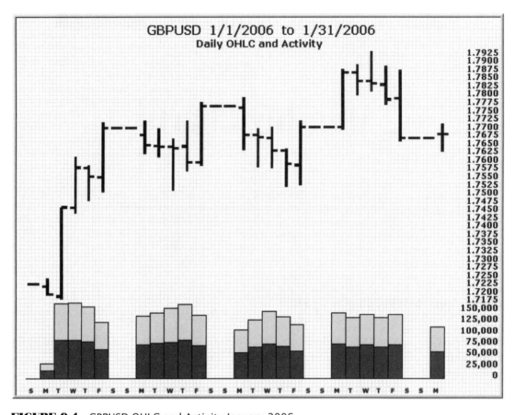

FIGURE 9.1   GBPUSD OHLC and Activity January 2006

GBPUSD Properties January 2006

Open	1.7232
High	1.7937
Low	1.7187
Close	1.7686
Mean	1.7660
Midrange	1.7562
Absolute Range	0.0750
Relative Range	4.2706
Standard Deviation	0.0149
Coefficient of Variation	0.8421

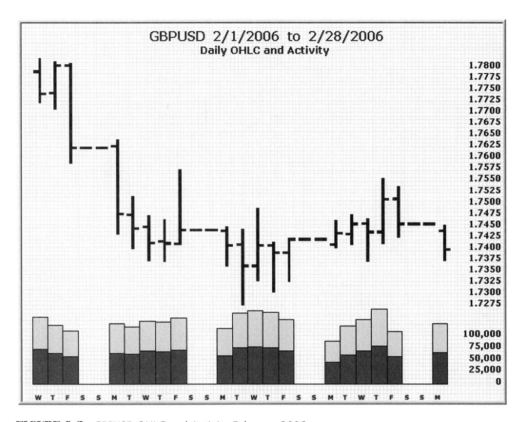

FIGURE 9.2 GBPUSD OHLC and Activity February 2006

GBPUSD Properties February 2006

Open	1.7793
High	0.7822
Low	1.7278
Close	1.7401
Mean	1.7480
Midrange	1.7550
Absolute Range	0.0544
Relative Range	3.0997
Standard Deviation	0.0109
Coefficient of Variation	0.6211

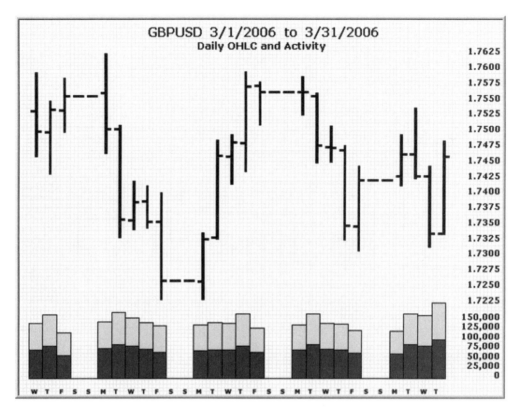

FIGURE 9.3 GBPUSD OHLC and Activity March 2006

GBPUSD Properties March 2006

Open	1.7534
High	1.7626
Low	1.7231
Close	1.7461
Mean	1.7449
Midrange	1.7429
Absolute Range	0.0395
Relative Range	2.2664
Standard Deviation	0.0100
Coefficient of Variation	0.5708

STATISTICS

The charts and tables yield the summary in the list below.

GBPUSD Properties January–March 2006

Month	High	Low	Mean	Rel Range	Coef Var
Jan	1.7937	1.7187	1.7660	4.2706	0.8421
Feb	1.7822	1.7278	1.7480	3.0997	0.6211
Mar	1.7626	1.7231	1.7449	2.9084	0.7332
Avg	1.2233	1.1828	1.2030	2.2664	0.5708

Composite Charts

DAILY COMPOSITE CHARTS

Refer to Chapter 2, Tools of the Trade, for a detailed description of both daily and weekly composite charts.

The time frame in the following charts (Figures 10.1 through 10.6) spans 1/1/2004 through 12/31/2005. Daily composite activity charts are calculated by averaging the sum of the upticks and downticks over that period using one-minute time intervals. Their purpose is to assist traders in determining when to schedule online trading sessions based upon traders' predilection to the nebulous risk/reward factor and the volatility of the targeted currency pair.

The vertical numeric scale on the right of each chart is activity expressed in total number of ticks (upticks plus downticks) during each time interval. The bottom band (the darkest) represents the activity for the current five-minute interval. The sum of both the upper and lower bands represents activity for the most recent ten-minute interval.

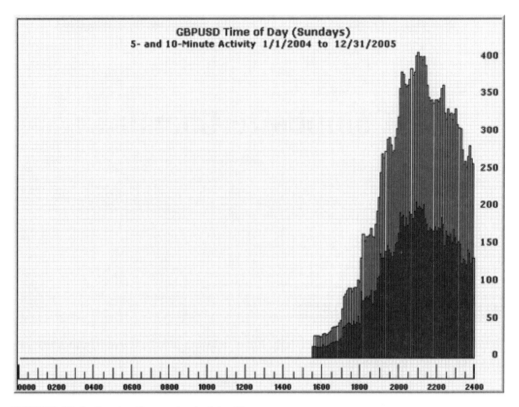

FIGURE 10.1 Sunday Composite Activity Chart

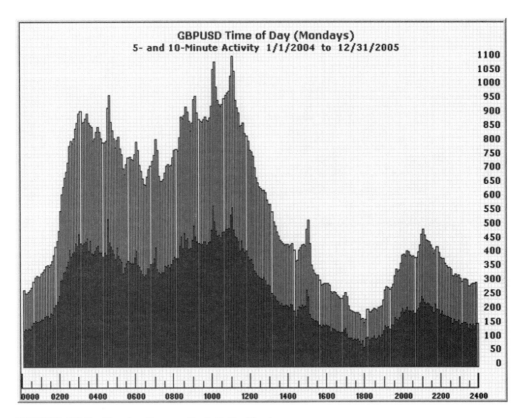

FIGURE 10.2 Monday Composite Activity Chart

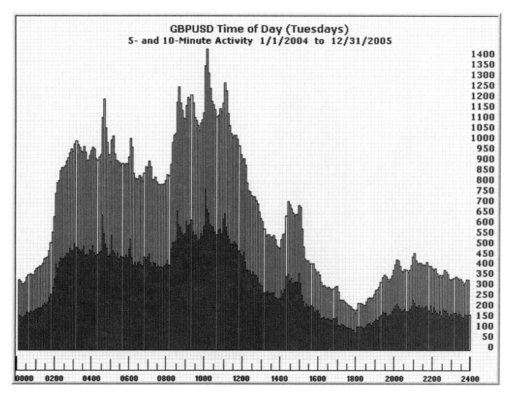

FIGURE 10.3 Tuesday Composite Activity Chart

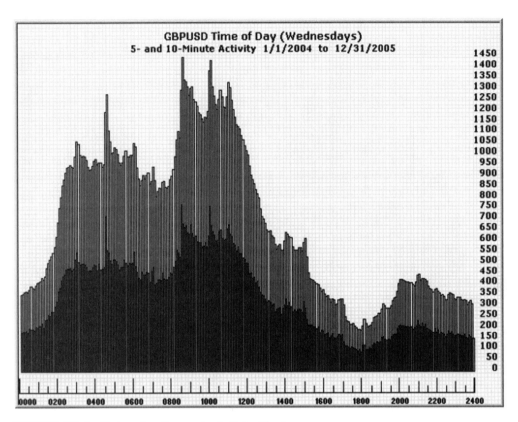

FIGURE 10.4 Wednesday Composite Activity Chart

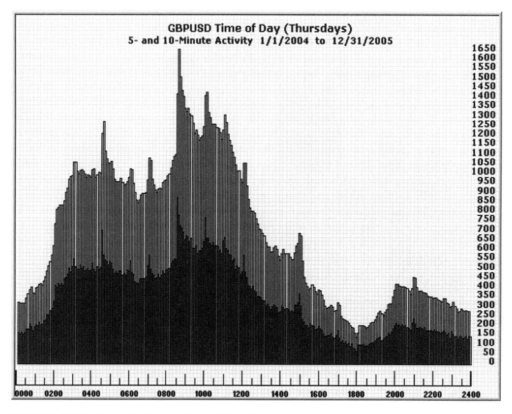

FIGURE 10.5 Thursday Composite Activity Chart

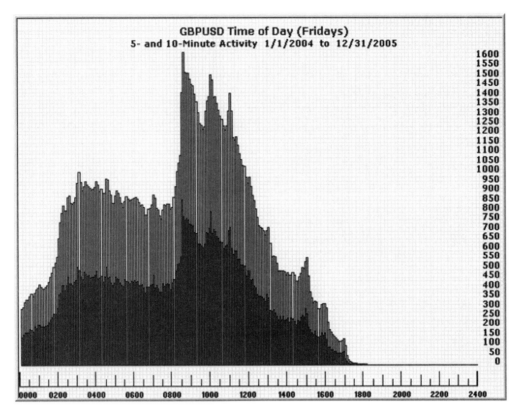

FIGURE 10.6 Friday Composite Activity Chart

WEEKLY COMPOSITE CHARTS

The following weekly composite (Figure 10.7) displays average hourly activity expressed in ticks (the sum of upticks plus downticks) for the two-year time frame 1/1/2004 through 12/31/2005.

The following weekly composite (Figure 10.8) displays average hourly range expressed as pips in the rightmost column for the two-year time frame 1/1/2004 through 12/31/2005.

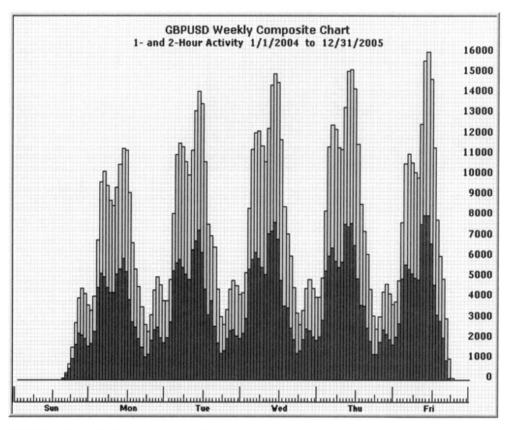

FIGURE 10.7 Weekly Composite Activity Chart

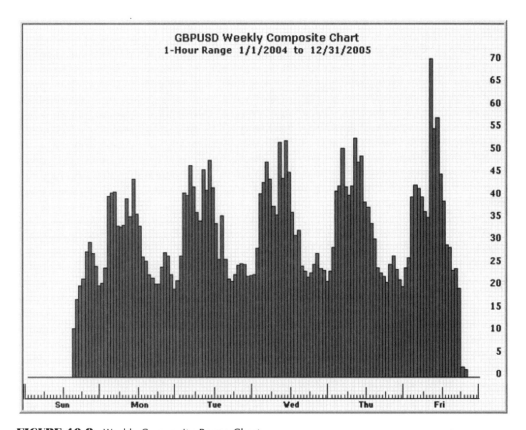

FIGURE 10.8 Weekly Composite Range Chart

By scrutinizing both the composite activity chart and the composite range chart for a specific currency pair, speculators can schedule their trading sessions according to their propensity toward overall volatility and risk factors.

PART IV

Swiss Franc

CHAPTER 11

History of the Swiss Franc

WHY TRADE THE SWISS FRANC?

With its long tradition of political and military neutrality, Switzerland holds a position of elevated respect in the arena of international banking and finance. Countries undergoing social and political uncertainty frequently convert liquid assets to the Swiss Franc in hopes of achieving a modicum of economic stability and security.

The International Standards Organization (ISO) symbol for the Swiss Franc is CHF which is an abbreviation for *Confoederatio Helvetica* (Latin for the Helvetian Confederation). This nomenclature avoids giving preference to any of the four official languages of Switzerland: German, French, Italian, and Romansh.

HISTORICAL PERSPECTIVE

The roots of modern Swiss sovereignty began in the 13th century. In 1291, the cantons of Uri, Schwyz, and Unterwalden conspired against the ruling Habsburgs. Their union is recorded in the Federal Charter, a document probably written after the fact. At the battles of Morgarten in 1315 and Sempach in 1386, the Swiss defeated the Habsburg army and secured a *de facto* independence.

By 1353, the three original cantons, joined by the cantons of Glarus and Zug and the city states of Lucerne, Zurich, and Berne, formed the "Old Federation" of eight states that persisted during much of the 15th century.

In 1518 Huldrych Zwingli was elected priest of the Great Minster church in Zurich. Zwingli's Reformation of 1523 was supported by the magistrate and population of Zürich and led to significant changes in civil life and state matters. The reformation spread from Zürich to five other cantons of Switzerland, while the remaining five sternly held onto the Roman Catholic faith, leading to intercantonal wars in 1529 and 1531.

The Thirty Years War (1618–1648), a religious conflict between Protestants and Catholics, was fought principally on the territory of current day Germany, but involved most of the major continental powers. During this period, Switzerland remained a relative oasis of peace and prosperity in war-torn Europe, mostly because all the major powers in Europe were depending on Swiss mercenaries, and they would not let Switzerland fall into the hands of one of their rivals. This is probably the first example of Swiss neutrality being enforced by outsiders. At the Treaty of Westphalia in 1648, Switzerland attained legal independence from the Holy Roman Empire.

During the French Revolutionary Wars, Napoleon's armies moved eastward through Switzerland in their battles against Austria. In 1798 Switzerland was completely overrun by the French and became the Helvetic Republic. The Congress of Vienna of 1815 fully reestablished Swiss independence, and the European powers agreed to permanently recognize Swiss neutrality.

During both World War I and World War II, Switzerland managed to maintain a position of armed neutrality and was not involved militarily. Switzerland reacted to Nazi Germany's invasion of Poland by a mobilization of some 430,000 troops. On May 11, 1940, the day following Hitler's attack on Belgium, general mobilization of the full army was ordered, which for the first time included some 15,000 women. Switzerland observed a restrictive immigration policy during the war, but nevertheless some 26,000 Jews and other refugees were granted asylum. Nazi Germany drew up plans to invade Switzerland, most notably "Operation Tannenbaum," but the invasion was never carried out.

In 1963, Switzerland joined the Council of Europe. Women were granted the right to vote only in 1971, and an equal rights amendment was ratified in 1981. In 1979, parts of the canton of Berne attained independence, forming the new canton of Jura.

Switzerland's role in many United Nations and international organizations helped to mitigate the country's concern for neutrality. In 2002, Switzerland was officially ratified as a member of the United Nations—the only country joining after agreement by a popular vote.

Switzerland is not a member state of the EU, but has been (together with Liechtenstein) surrounded by EU territory since Austria joined the EU in 1995.

In 2005, Switzerland agreed by popular vote to join the Schengen Treaty (an agreement among European states that allows for common immigration policies and a border system) and the Dublin Convention (a European Union law to streamline the application process for refugees seeking political asylum under the Geneva Convention).

The Swiss Franc has historically been considered a safe haven currency with virtually zero inflation and a legal requirement that a minimum 40 percent is backed by gold reserves. However, this link to gold, which dates from the 1920s, was terminated on May 1, 2000, following an amendment to the Swiss Constitution. The Swiss Franc has suffered devaluation only once, on September 27, 1936, during the Great Depression, when the currency was devalued by 30 percent following the devaluations of the British Pound, U.S. Dollar and French Franc.

BANKNOTES AND COINS

Since 1907, when the first series of Swiss banknotes was printed, eight series have been printed, six of which have been released for use by the general public. The current (8th) series of banknotes was designed by Jörg Zintzmeyer around the theme of the arts and was released starting in 1995. (See Figures 11.1 and 11.2.)

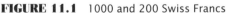

FIGURE 11.1   1000 and 200 Swiss Francs

FIGURE 11.2   100 and 50 Swiss Francs

The first Swiss coins were released in 1850. Before this date, the different Swiss cantons had their own money, with different names and values. (See Table 11.1.)

In addition to these general circulation coins, numerous series of commemorative coins have been issued, as well as gold coins including the well-known Vreneli. These coins generally remain legal tender, but are not used as such because their material or collector's value usually exceeds their face value. (See Figures 11.3 through 11.5.)

TABLE 11.1 Overview of Current Swiss Coins

Value	Diameter(mm)	Thickness(mm)	Weight(g)	Alloy
1 centime	16.00	1.10	1.5	Bronze
5 centimes	17.15	1.25	1.8	Aluminum bronze
10 centimes	19.15	1.45	3.0	Cupronickel
20 centimes	21.05	1.65	4.0	Cupronickel
50 centimes	18.20	1.25	2.2	Cupronickel (silver until 1967)
1 franc	23.20	1.55	4.4	Cupronickel (silver until 1967)
2 francs	27.40	2.15	8.8	Cupronickel (silver until 1967)
5 francs	31.45	2.35	13.2	Cupronickel (silver until 1967)

FIGURE 11.3 Five Swiss Francs—Obverse and Reverse

FIGURE 11.4 Two Swiss Francs—Obverse and Reverse

FIGURE 11.5   One Swiss Franc—Obverse and Reverse

For additional details, visit http://en.wikipedia.org.

CHAPTER 12

Annual Charts

OHLC AND ACTIVITY CHARTS

In this chapter, we examine historical charts for the years 2000 through 2005 using daily interval data. In the lower portion of each chart, activity is expressed in terms of ticks of the currency pair. (See Figures 12.1 through 12.7.)

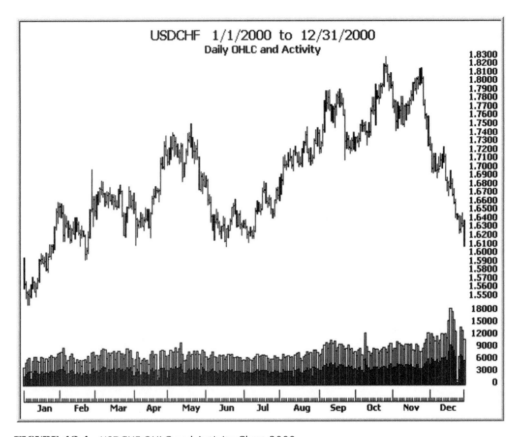

FIGURE 12.1 USDCHF OHLC and Activity Chart 2000

USDCHF Properties 2000

Open	1.5908
High	1.8309
Low	1.5427
Close	1.6111
Midrange	1.6868
Absolute Range	0.2882
Relative Range	17.0856
Arithmetic Mean	1.6889
Standard Deviation	0.0610
Coefficient of Variation	3.6121

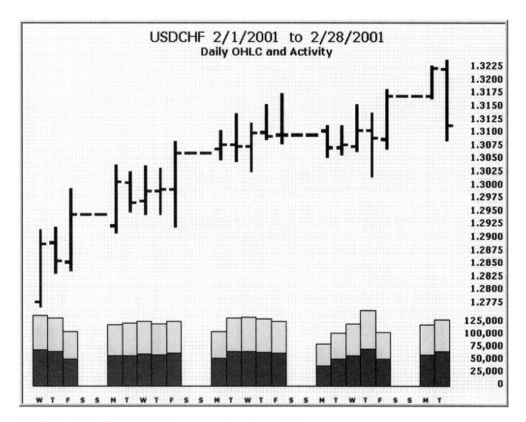

FIGURE 12.2 USDCHF OHLC and Activity Chart 2001

USDCHF Properties 2001

Open	1.6105
High	1.8226
Low	1.5675
Close	0.6616
Midrange	1.6951
Absolute Range	0.2551
Relative Range	15.0497
Arithmetic Mean	1.6871
Standard Deviation	0.0558
Coefficient of Variation	3.3049

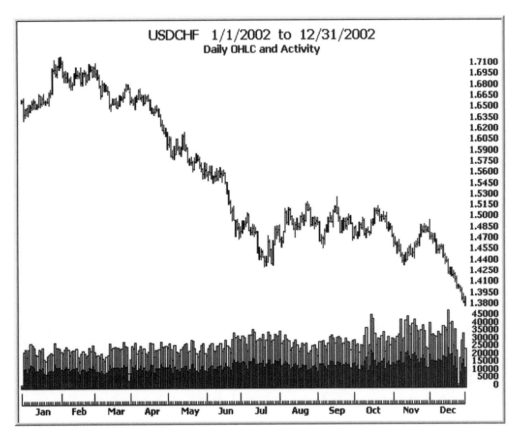

FIGURE 12.3   USDCHF OHLC and Activity Chart 2002

USDCHF Properties 2002

Open	1.6616
High	1.7229
Low	1.3805
Close	1.3824
Midrange	1.5517
Absolute Range	0.3424
Relative Range	22.0661
Arithmetic Mean	1.5553
Standard Deviation	0.0924
Coefficient of Variation	5.9419

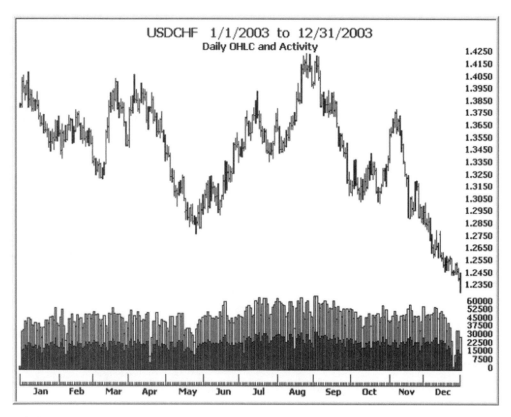

FIGURE 12.4 USDCHF OHLC and Activity Chart 2003

USDCHF Properties 2003

Open	1.3824
High	1.4254
Low	1.2310
Close	1.2390
Midrange	1.3282
Absolute Range	0.1944
Relative Range	14.6363
Arithmetic Mean	1.3443
Standard Deviation	0.0398
Coefficient of Variation	2.9632

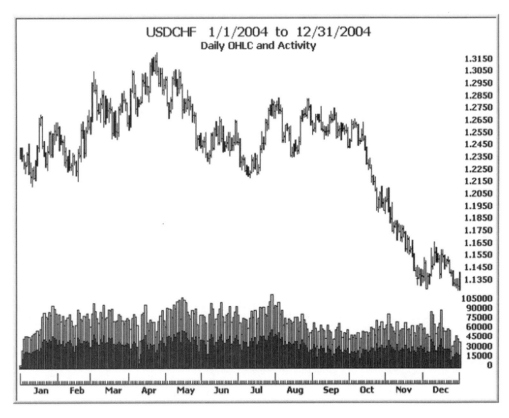

FIGURE 12.5   USDCHF OHLC and Activity Chart 2004

USDCHF Properties 2004

Open	1.2384
High	1.3226
Low	1.1288
Close	1.1392
Midrange	1.2257
Absolute Range	0.1938
Relative Range	15.8114
Arithmetic Mean	1.2419
Standard Deviation	0.0450
Coefficient of Variation	3.6251

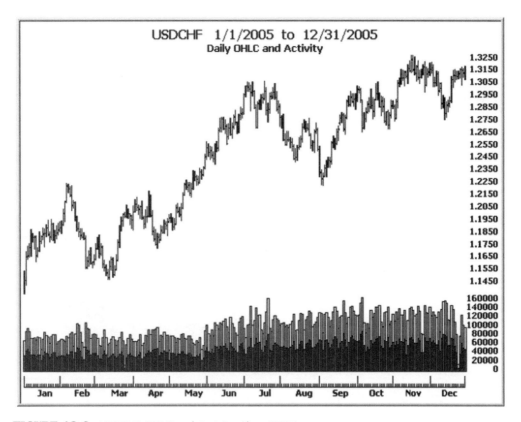

FIGURE 12.6 USDCHF OHLC and Activity Chart 2005

USDCHF Properties 2005

Open	1.1401
High	1.3287
Low	1.1372
Close	1.3136
Midrange	1.2330
Absolute Range	0.1915
Relative Range	15.5319
Arithmetic Mean	1.2461
Standard Deviation	0.0505
Coefficient of Variation	4.0515

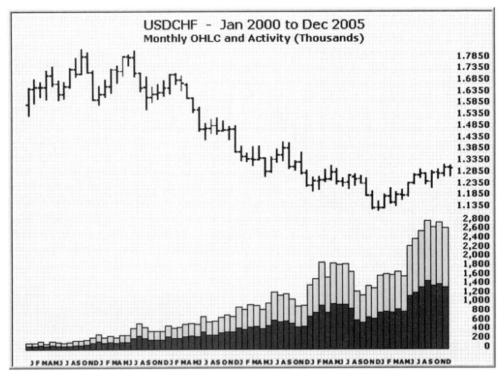

FIGURE 12.7 USDCHF OHLC and Activity Chart 2000–2005

STATISTICS

USDCHF Properties 2000–2005

Year	High	Low	Mean	Rel Range	Coef Var
2000	1.8309	1.5427	1.6889	17.0856	3.6121
2001	1.8226	1.5675	1.6871	15.0497	3.3049
2002	1.7229	1.3805	1.5553	22.0661	5.9419
2003	1.4254	1.2310	1.3443	14.6363	2.9632
2004	1.3226	1.1288	1.2419	15.8114	3.6251
2005	1.3287	1.1372	1.2461	15.5319	4.0398
Avg	1.5755	1.3704	1.4606	16.6968	3.9145

Monthly Charts

OHLC AND ACTIVITY CHARTS

In the current chapter, we examine recent market behavior in the USDCHF currency pair for the months January through March 2006 using daily interval data. (See Figures 13.1 through 13.3.)

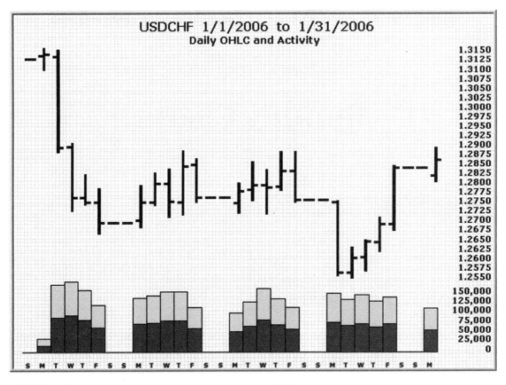

FIGURE 13.1   USDCHF OHLC and Activity January 2006

USDCHF Properties January 2006

Open	1.3136
High	1.3164
Low	1.2556
Close	1.2869
Mean	1.2792
Midrange	1.2860
Absolute Range	0.0608
Relative Range	4.7278
Standard Deviation	0.0121
Coefficient of Variation	0.9440

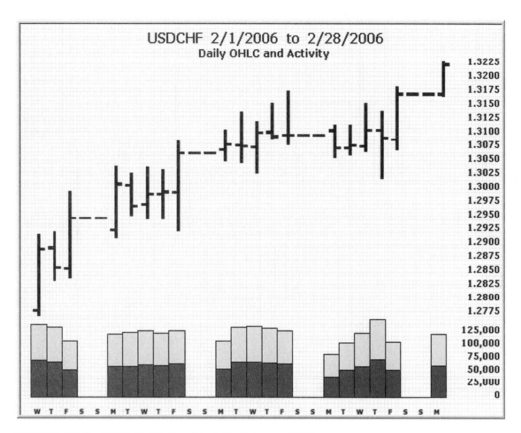

FIGURE 13.2 USDCHF OHLC and Activity February 2006

USDCHF Properties February 2006

Open	1.2781
High	1.3231
Low	1.2772
Close	1.3226
Mean	1.3056
Midrange	1.3002
Absolute Range	0.0459
Relative Range	3.5304
Standard Deviation	0.0088
Coefficient of Variation:	0.6778

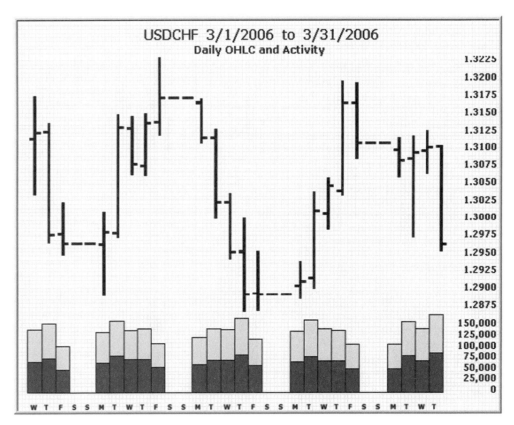

FIGURE 13.3   USDCHF OHLC and Activity March 2006

USDCHF Properties March 2006

Open	1.3117
High	1.3232
Low	1.2871
Close	1.2967
Mean	1.3043
Midrange	1.3052
Absolute Range	0.0361
Relative Range	2.7660
Standard Deviation	0.0096
Coefficient of Variation:	0.7348

STATISTICS

USDCHF Properties January–March 2006

Month	High	Low	Mean	Rel Range	Coef Var
Jan	1.3164	1.1801	1.2792	4.7278	0.9440
Feb	1.3231	1.2772	1.3056	3.5304	0.6778
Mar	1.3232	1.2871	1.3043	2.7660	0.7332
Avg	1.3209	1.2481	1.2963	3.6747	0.7348

Composite Charts

DAILY COMPOSITE CHARTS

See Chapter 2, Tools of the Trade, for a detailed description of both daily and weekly composite charts

The time frame in the following charts spans 1/1/2005 through 4/14/2006. (See Figures 14.1 through 14.8.) Daily composite activity charts are calculated by averaging the sum of the upticks and downticks over that period using one-minute time intervals. Their purpose is to assist traders in determining when to schedule online trading sessions based upon traders' predilection to the nebulous risk/reward factor and the volatility of the targeted currency pair.

The vertical numeric scale on the right of each chart is activity expressed in total number of ticks (upticks plus downticks) during each time interval. The bottom band (the darkest) represents the activity for the current five-minute interval. The sum of the lower and upper bands represents ten-minute activity.

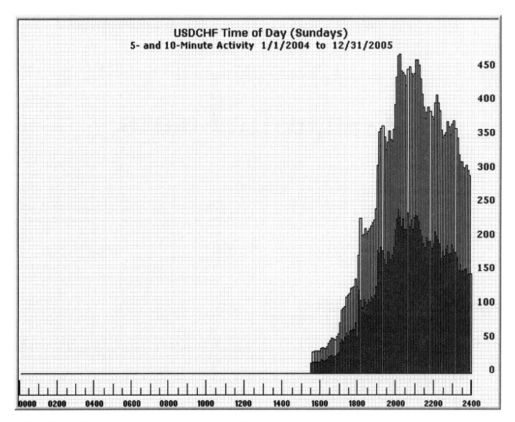

FIGURE 14.1 Sunday Composite Activity Chart

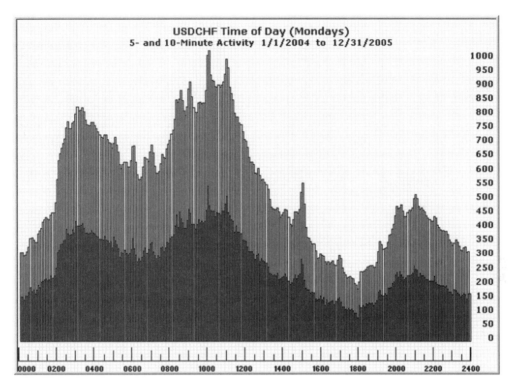

FIGURE 14.2 Monday Composite Activity Chart

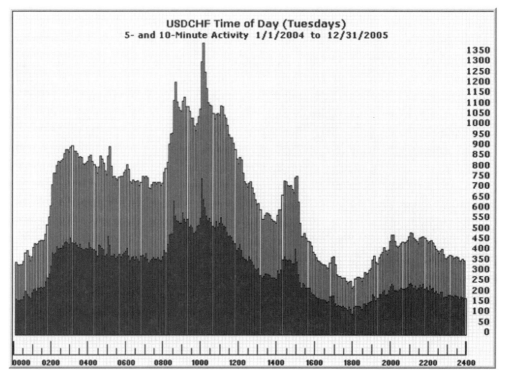

FIGURE 14.3 Tuesday Composite Activity Chart

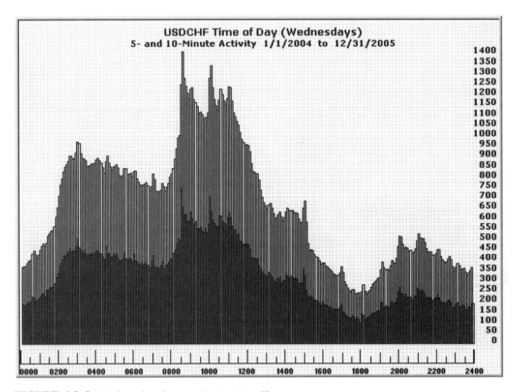

FIGURE 14.4 Wednesday Composite Activity Chart

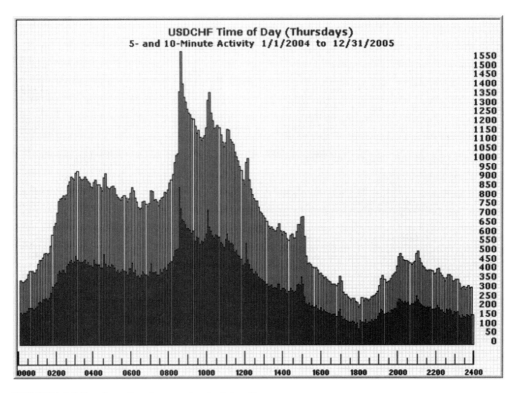

FIGURE 14.5   Thursday Composite Activity Chart

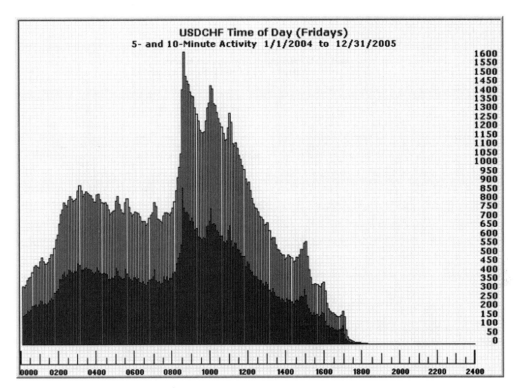

FIGURE 14.6   Friday Composite Activity Chart

WEEKLY COMPOSITE CHARTS

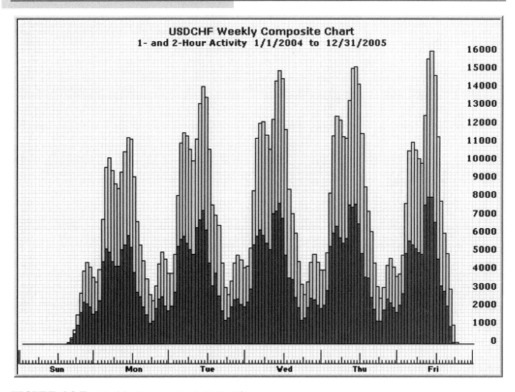

FIGURE 14.7 Weekly Composite Activity Chart

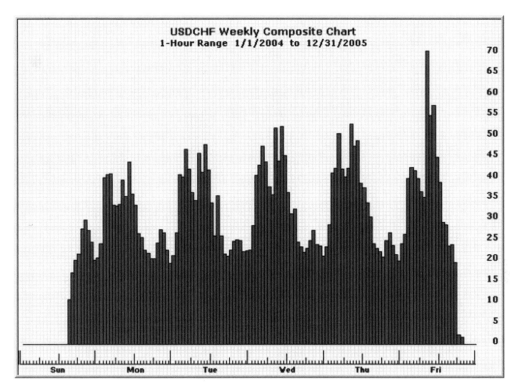

FIGURE 14.8 Weekly Composite Range Chart

PART V

Japanese Yen

CHAPTER 15

History of the Japanese Yen

WHY TRADE THE YEN?

The Japanese economy is one of the strongest in the world. Only the United States has a higher Gross Domestic Product. Japan's main export goods are cars, electronic devices, and computers. The most important single trade partner is the United States, which imports more than one-quarter of all Japanese exports. Other major export countries are Taiwan, Hong Kong, South Korea, China, and Singapore.

Japan has a large surplus in its export/import balance. The most important import goods are raw materials such as oil, foodstuffs, and wood. Major suppliers are the United States, China, Indonesia, South Korea, and Australia. Manufacturing, construction, distribution, real estate, services, and communication are Japan's major industries today. Agriculture makes up only about 2 percent of the GNP. The most important agricultural product is rice. Resources of raw materials are very limited and the mining industry rather small.

HISTORICAL PERSPECTIVE

The history of Japan is lost in legend, and reliable records date back only to about A.D. 400. Korean invaders probably introduced bronze and iron implements around the first century. Portuguese sailors made the first European contact with Japan in 1542. Commercial trading with the West developed gradually but only on a very limited scale.

The Yen was established as the official unit of currency in 1871 by order of the Meiji government. The Bank of Japan, established in 1882, issued its first Yen bank notes in 1885.

In 1945, in accordance with the emergency measures intended to suppress the post-war hyperinflation, the Japanese people were obligated to deposit their money by a certain date in monetary institutions for a specific period of time. Banknotes then in circulation were made invalid. Withdrawal of the frozen deposits in the form of the new banknotes was then allowed to a limited extent. But not enough new banknotes were printed for withdrawal. To cope with this, existing banknotes with adhesive stickers were regarded as new banknotes and circulated until the end of October in that year as a makeshift arrangement.

Japan's economy crashed as a result of defeat by the Allies, causing a 49.6 billion Yen loss due to wartime damages. The total reached 1.38 trillion Yen by the end of 1947 (equal to 20 percent of Japan's pre-war domestic assets). National income dropped to 6.5 million Yen.

In 1946 the Economic Stabilization Board was established, which put almost all sectors of the national economy (commodities, prices, transport, banking, etc.) under the systematic control of the board. In October the Reconstruction Finance Bank was established, which furnished enormous volumes of funds to industries vital to economic recovery, such as the coal, steel, and chemical fertilizer industries.

In 1949 Joseph Dodge, the economic advisor to the General Headquarters of the Allied Occupation Forces, mapped out the Dodge Line Policy to promote a self-sustaining economy. This plan established a single exchange rate for the Yen and attempted to stabilize the currency as well as close the gap between domestic and overseas prices in general. It also curtailed government spending with a tight-money policy. By this time, the exchange rate had risen to 360 Yen to the U.S. dollar.

During the Korean War (1950–1953), special procurement contracts by the American government for goods and services generated $315 million for Japan. During this time period, Japan attempted to reduce dependence on imports by increasing modernization of processing in the four major industries (steel, coal, etc.), importing new technologies, and improving on old ones (synthetic fibers and petrochemicals). Japan's foreign exchange reserves quadrupled from $260 million in 1949 to $1.06 billion in 1951. In 1953 Japanese exports were 50 percent greater than before the Korean War. Domestic prices rose in response to the increase in export and import prices.

Due to a drop in exports from 1963 to 1965, Japan experienced another recession. The government issued long-term public bonds. Foreign exchange reserves remained stable at about $2 billion. From 1965 to 1970, the Japanese economy began to prosper. Average growth rate of the economy remained stable at 11.8 percent for these five years. Today, Japan has the second highest GNP in the world behind the United States.

In 1971 Japan's foreign exchange reserves reached $15.2 billion. Modernization of industrial equipment over the past 10 years resulted in better prices and more efficient production of goods. The Bretton Woods system of fixed exchange rates for currency worldwide collapsed as a result of the devaluation of the U.S. dollar. President Nixon enacted an emergency policy that applied a 10 percent surcharge to imports to the United States and also suspended the conversion of the U.S. dollar into gold.

The Smithsonian floating exchange rates for worldwide currencies were implemented in 1973. The Japanese Yen was revalued against the U.S. dollar at a lower rate, causing an increase in imports into Japan due to cheaper import prices. In the same year war broke out in the Middle East, the export of crude oil was temporarily suspended, and oil prices increased worldwide. Japan was one of the many nations that underwent severe recession due to the oil crisis and collapse of the fixed exchange rate system. In 1979 a second oil crisis broke out, and plunged Japan from a positive $13.9 billion to a $7 billion deficit by 1980. (See Table 15.1 and Figure 15.1.)

The rise of the Japanese Yen from 1971 to the present is one of the most dramatic economic phenomena in recent years. This fact alone makes it a prime Forex trading candidate. Additionally, the trading volume of the Yen at the Chicago Mercantile Exchange is exceeded only by the Euro currency. Further historical information on the Yen can be found at http://www.imes.boj.or.jp.

TABLE 15.1   USDJPY 1948 to 2004

Year	USDJPY	Year	USDJPY	Year	USDJPY
1948	201.61	1967	360.01	1986	168.52
1949	314.47	1968	360.00	1987	144.63
1950	361.10	1969	360.00	1988	128.15
1951	361.10	1970	360.00	1989	137.97
1952	361.10	1971	350.67	1990	144.80
1953	360.00	1972	303.17	1991	134.71
1954	360.00	1973	271.70	1992	126.65
1955	360.00	1974	292.08	1993	111.19
1956	360.00	1975	296.79	1994	102.21
1957	360.00	1976	296.56	1995	100.40
1958	360.00	1977	268.50	1996	108.77
1959	360.00	1978	210.45	1997	120.99
1960	360.00	1979	219.14	1998	130.90
1961	360.00	1980	226.74	1999	113.91
1962	360.00	1981	220.03	2000	107.77
1963	360.00	1982	249.08	2001	121.53
1964	360.00	1983	237.51	2002	125.40
1965	360.00	1984	237.52	2003	115.94
1966	360.00	1985	238.53	2004	108.19

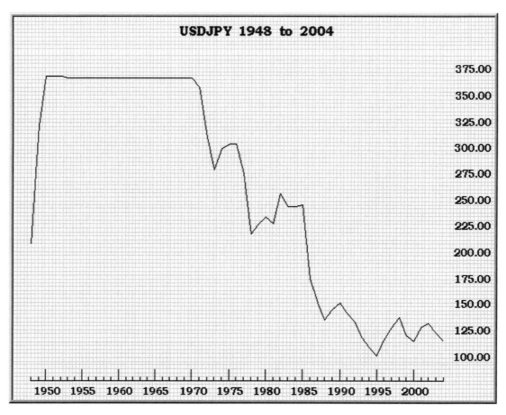

FIGURE 15.1   USDJPY 1948 to 2004

BANKNOTES AND COINS

The Japanese currency is the Yen, which literally means "circle" since the previous coinage was oblong. One Yen corresponds to 100 sen. However, sen are not used in everyday life anymore. Coins come in 1 Yen, 5 Yen, 10 Yen, 50 Yen, 100 Yen and 500 Yen. Bank note denominations are 1000 Yen, 2000 Yen, 5000 Yen, and 10000 Yen. (See Figures 15.2 and 15.3.)

FIGURE 15.2   2000 Yen Banknote

FIGURE 15.3   Yen Coins (1, 5, 10, 50, 100, and 500)

CHAPTER 16

Annual Charts

OHLC AND ACTIVITY CHARTS

Figures 16.1 through 16.7 show the annual USDJPY charts for the years 2000 through 2005.

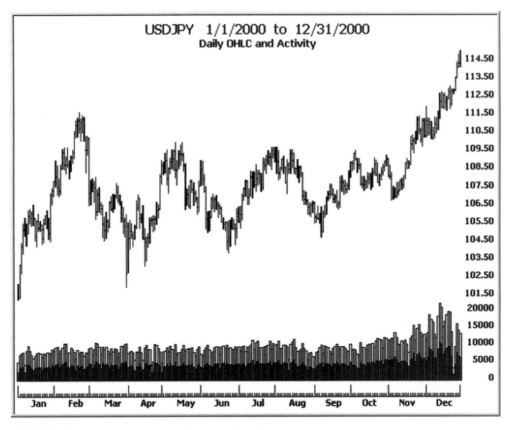

FIGURE 16.1 USDJPY OHLC and Activity Chart 2000

USDJPY Properties 2000

Open	102.2100
High	115.0800
Low	101.3600
Close	114.3900
Midrange	108.2200
Absolute Range	13.7200
Relative Range	12.6779
Arithmetic Mean	107.8082
Standard Deviation	2.1073
Coefficient of Variation	1.9546

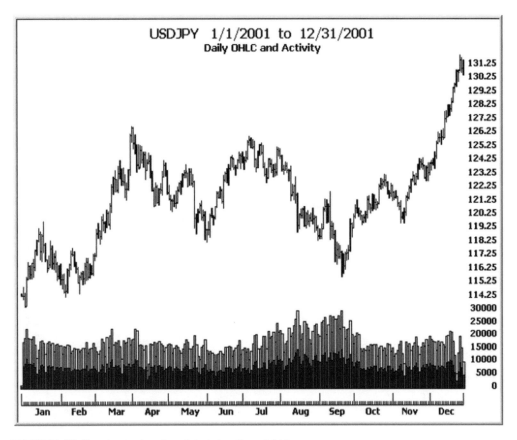

FIGURE 16.2 USDJPY OHLC and Activity Chart 2001

USDJPY Properties 2001

Open	114.3900
High	132.0500
Low	113.6000
Close	131.6200
Midrange	122.8250
Absolute Range	18.4500
Relative Range	15.0214
Arithmetic Mean	121.5169
Standard Deviation	3.3926
Coefficient of Variation	2.7918

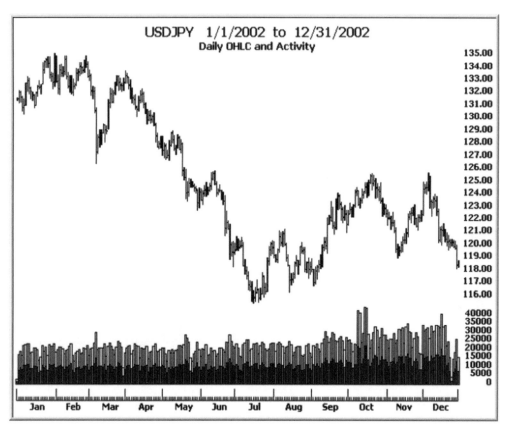

FIGURE 16.3   USDJPY OHLC and Activity Chart 2002

USDJPY Properties 2002

Open	131.6200
High	135.1600
Low	115.4900
Close	118.8000
Midrange	125.3250
Absolute Range	19.6700
Relative Range	15.6952
Arithmetic Mean	125.2000
Standard Deviation	5.4791
Coefficient of Variation	4.3763

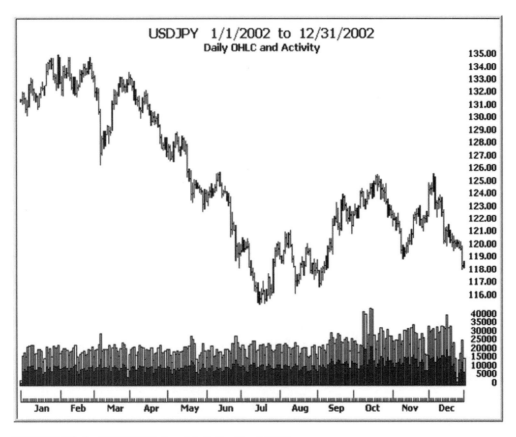

FIGURE 16.4 USDJPY OHLC and Activity Chart 2003

USDJPY Properties 2003

Open	118.7600
High	121.8900
Low	106.7000
Close	107.2200
Midrange	114.2950
Absolute Range	15.1900
Relative Range	13.2902
Arithmetic Mean	115.8766
Standard Deviation	4.4659
Coefficient of Variation	3.8540

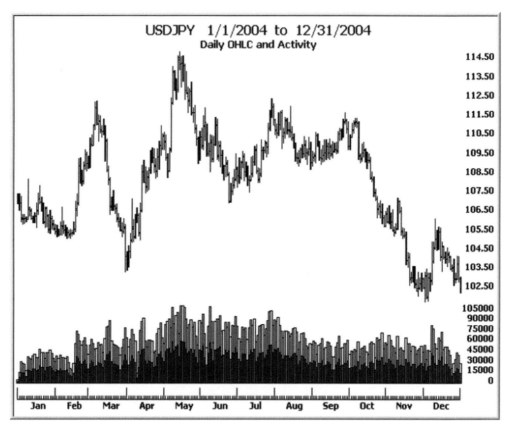

FIGURE 16.5   USDJPY OHLC and Activity Chart 2004

USDJPY Properties 2004

Open	107.2000
High	114.9200
Low	101.8500
Close	102.5200
Midrange	108.3850
Absolute Range	13.0700
Relative Range	12.0589
Arithmetic Mean	108.1089
Standard Deviation	2.7194
Coefficient of Variation	2.5154

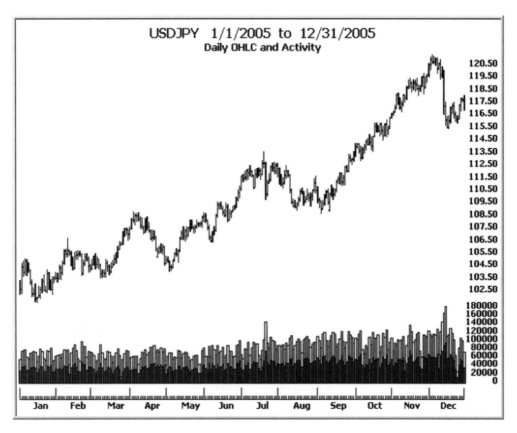

FIGURE 16.6 USDJPY OHLC and Activity Chart 2005

USDJPY Properties 2005

Open	102.6100
High	121.4200
Low	101.7000
Close	117.7500
Midrange	111.5600
Absolute Range	19.7200
Relative Range	17.6766
Arithmetic Mean	110.1595
Standard Deviation	4.9922
Coefficient of Variation	4.5318

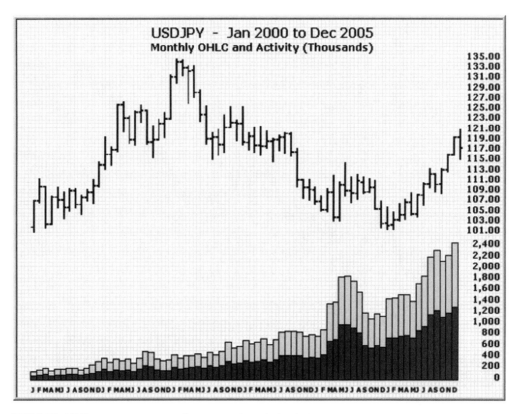

FIGURE 16.7   USDJPY OHLC and Activity Chart 2000–2005

STATISTICS

USDJPY Properties 2000-2005

Year	High	Low	Mean	Rel Range	Coef Var
2000	115.08	101.36	107.81	12.6779	1.9546
2001	132.05	113.60	121.52	15.0214	2.7918
2002	135.16	115.49	125.20	15.6952	4.3763
2003	121.89	106.70	115.87	13.2902	3.8540
2004	114.92	101.85	108.11	12.0589	2.5154
2005	121.42	101.70	110.16	17.6766	4.5318
All	135.16	101.36	115.18	28.5811	7.0637

CHAPTER 17

Monthly Charts

OHLC AND ACTIVITY CHARTS

In the current chapter, we examine recent market behavior in the USDJPY currency pair for the months January through March 2006 using daily interval data. (See Figures 17.1 through 17.4.)

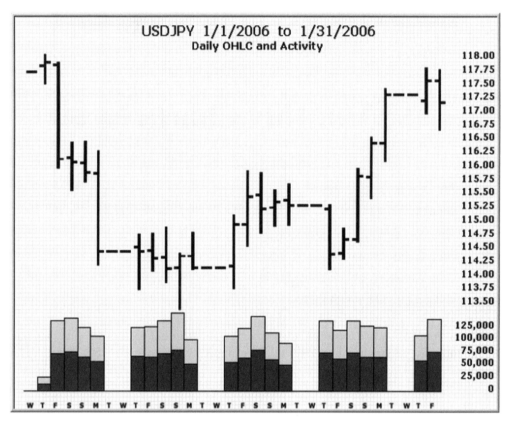

FIGURE 17.1   USDJPY OHLC and Activity January 2006

USDJPY Properties January 2006

Open	117.7500
High	118.0700
Low	113.4100
Close	117.2000
Mean	115.5606
Midrange	115.7400
Absolute Range	4.6600
Relative Range	4.0263
Standard Deviation	1.2478
Coefficient of Variation	1.0798

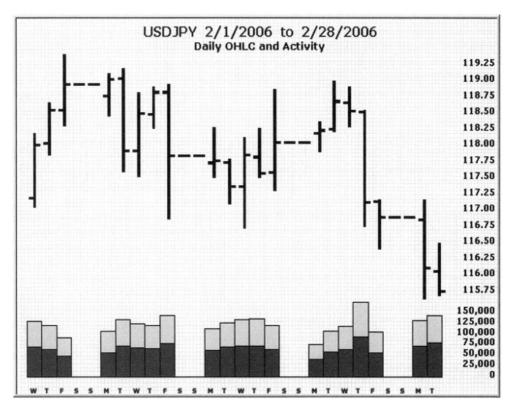

FIGURE 17.2 USDJPY OHLC and Activity February 2006

USDJPY Properties February 2006

Open	117.2100
High	119.4200
Low	115.6600
Close	115.7700
Mean	117.9104
Midrange	117.5400
Absolute Range	3.7600
Relative Range	3.1989
Standard Deviation	0.8436
Coefficient of Variation	0.7154

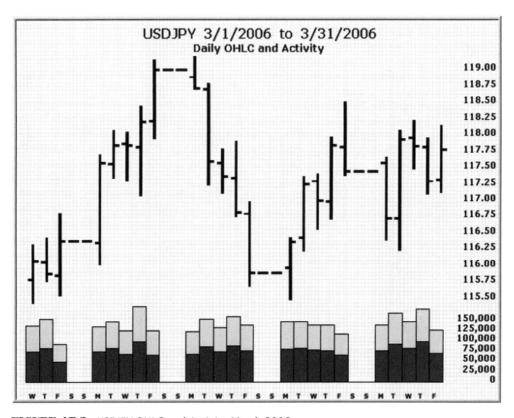

FIGURE 17.3 USDJPY OHLC and Activity March 2006

USDJPY Properties March 2006

Open	115.8000
High	119.2100
Low	115.4500
Close	117.7900
Mean	117.3061
Midrange	117.3300
Absolute Range	3.7600
Relative Range	3.2046
Standard Deviation	0.9489
Coefficient of Variation	0.8089

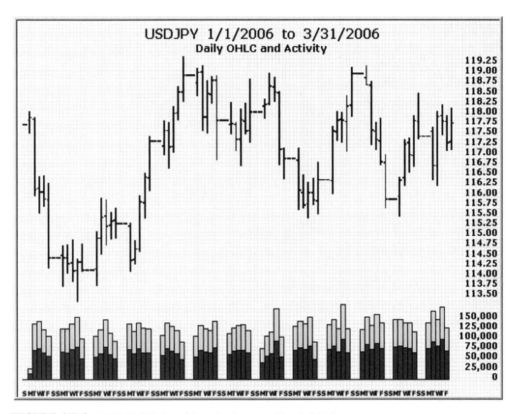

FIGURE 17.4 USDJPY OHLC and Activity January–March 2006

USDJPY Properties January–March 2006

Open	117.7500
High	119.4200
Low	113.4100
Close	117.7900
Mean	116.8929
Midrange	116.4150
Absolute Range	6.0100
Relative Range	5.1626
Standard Deviation	1.4310
Coefficient of Variation	1.2242

STATISTICS

USDJPY Properties January–March 2006

Month	High	Low	Mean	Rel Range	Coef Var
Jan	118.07	113.41	115.56	4.0263	1.0798
Feb	119.42	115.66	117.91	3.1989	0.7154
Mar	119.21	115.45	117.31	3.2046	0.8089
All	119.42	113.41	116.89	5.1626	1.2242

Composite Charts

DAILY COMPOSITE CHARTS

See Chapter 2, Tools of the Trade, for a detailed description of both daily and weekly composite charts

The time frame in the following charts spans 1/1/2004 through 12/31/2005. (See Figures 18.1 through 18.8.) Daily composite activity charts are calculated by averaging the sum of the upticks and downticks over that period using one-minute time intervals. Their purpose is to assist traders in determining when to schedule online trading sessions based upon traders' predilection to the nebulous risk/reward factor and the volatility of the targeted currency pair.

The vertical numeric scale on the right of each chart is activity expressed in total number of ticks (upticks plus downticks) during each time interval. The bottom band (the darkest) represents the activity for the current five-minute interval. The sum of the lower and upper bands represents ten-minute activity.

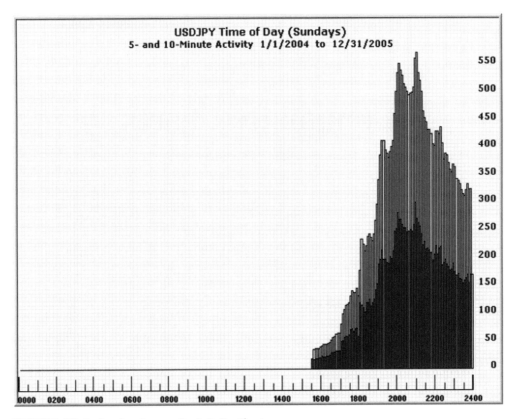

FIGURE 18.1 Sunday Composite Activity Chart

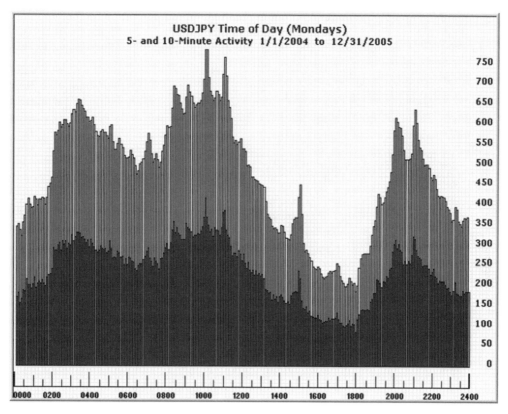

FIGURE 18.2 Monday Composite Activity Chart

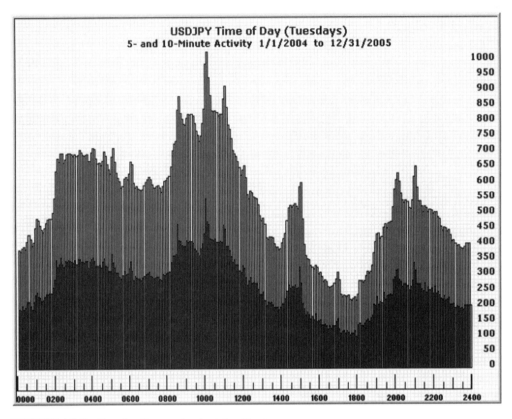

FIGURE 18.3 Tuesday Composite Activity Chart

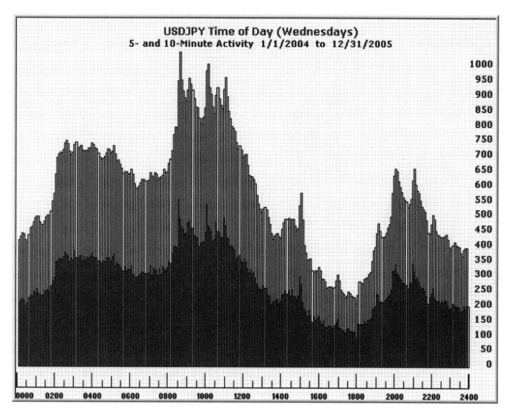

FIGURE 18.4 Wednesday Composite Activity Chart

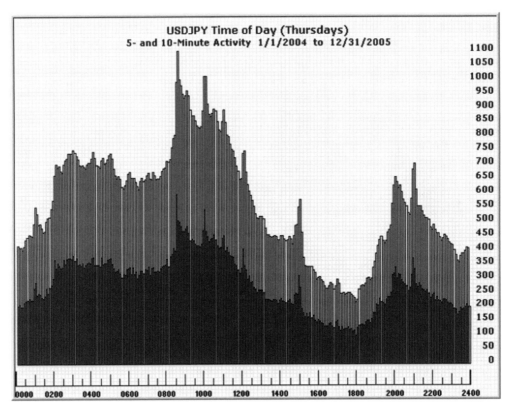

FIGURE 18.5 Thursday Composite Activity Chart

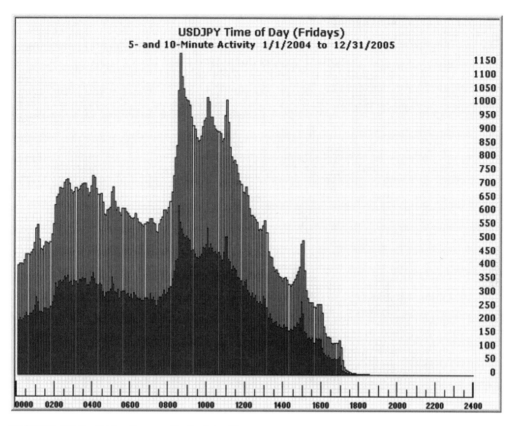

FIGURE 18.6 Friday Composite Activity Chart

WEEKLY COMPOSITE CHARTS

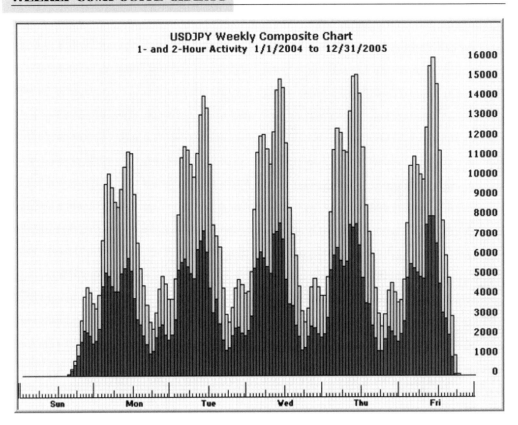

FIGURE 18.7   Weekly Composite Activity Chart

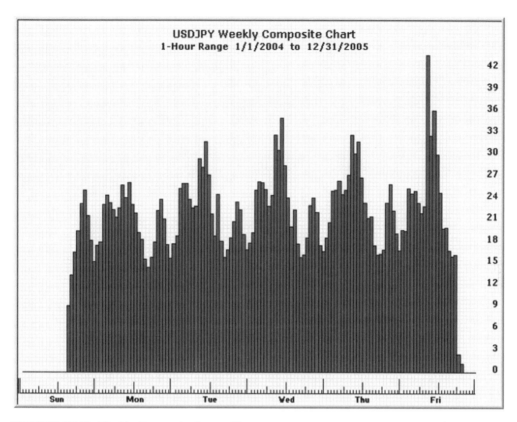

FIGURE 18.8 Weekly Composite Range Chart

PART VI

Cross Rates

CHAPTER 19

Cross Rates Charts

OVERVIEW

A *cross rate* is any currency pair in which neither the base currency nor the quote currency is the U.S. Dollar. For example, a long position in the British Pound with a simultaneous short in the Swiss Franc is a cross rate. Obviously. this definition is relative. When trading Forex markets in Tokyo, the EURUSD currency pair is considered a cross rate.

Cross rate futures provide a way for banks, corporations, money managers, and individuals with the tools to manage the risks associated with currency rate fluctuation and to take advantage of profit opportunities stemming from changes in currency rates. Currency cross rate futures are physically delivered at expiration. Exercised options contracts are settled by the delivery of futures contracts. Presently, the Chicago Mercantile Exchange offers the cross rate contracts shown in Table 19.1.

TABLE 19.1 CME Cross Rate Futures
Australian Dollar/Canadian Dollar
Australian Dollar/New Zealand Dollar
Australian Dollar/Japanese Yen
British Pound/Swiss Franc
British Pound/Japanese Yen
Canadian Dollar/Japanese Yen
Euro/Australian Dollar
Euro/British Pound
Euro/Canadian Dollar
Euro/Czech Koruna
Euro/Hungarian Forint
Euro/Japanese Yen
Euro/Norwegian Krone
Euro/Polish Zloty
Euro/Swedish Krona
Euro/Swiss Franc
Swiss Franc/Japanese Yen

Visit http://www.cme.com/trading/prd/fx/crossrate2625.html for additional information.

In the analysis below, we will restrict ourselves to those cross rates involving the major currencies EUR, GBP, CHF, and JPY.

MONTHLY OHLC AND ACTIVITY CHARTS

This section uses the time frame 1/1/2000 to 12/31/2005 as the basis for monthly OHLC and activity charts in the six cross rate currency pairs. (See Figures 19.1 through 19.6.)

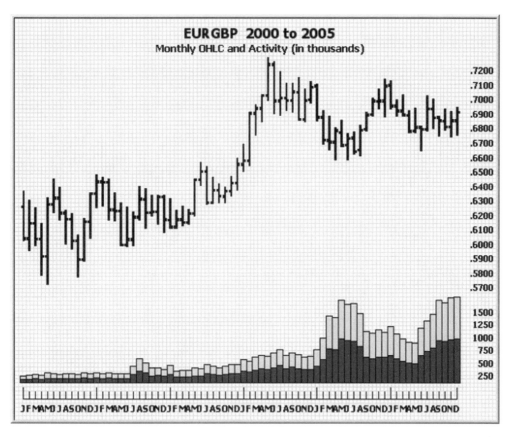

FIGURE 19.1 EURGBP OHLC and Activity Chart 2000–2005

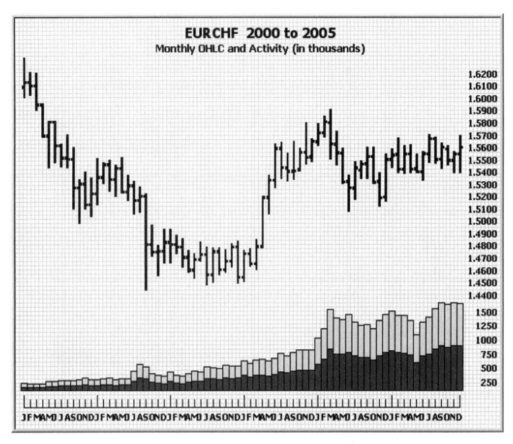

FIGURE 19.2 EURCHF OHLC and Activity Chart 2000–2005

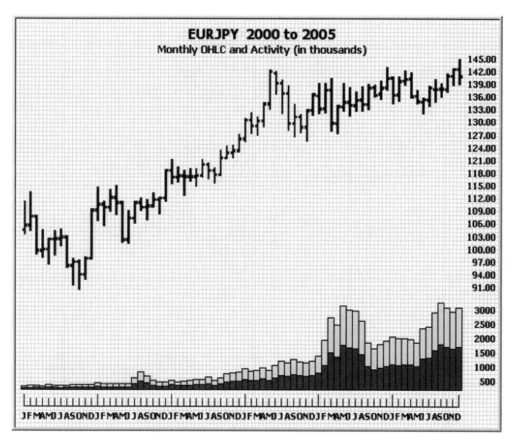

FIGURE 19.3 EURJPY OHLC and Activity Chart 2000–2005

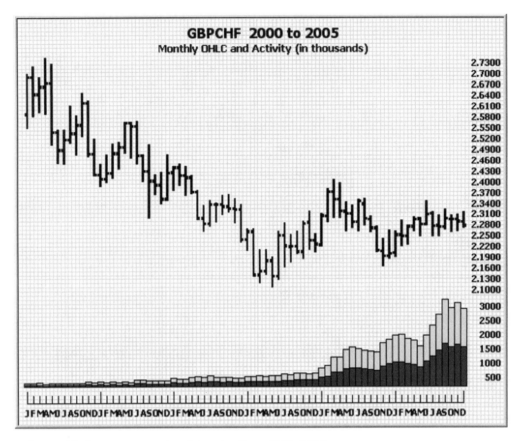

FIGURE 19.4 GBPCHF OHLC and Activity Chart 2000–2005

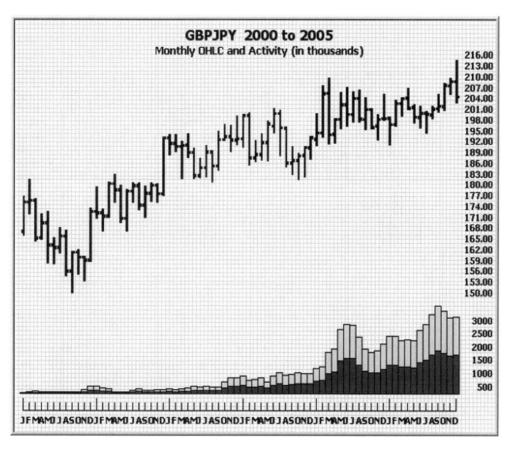

FIGURE 19.5 GBPJPY OHLC and Activity Chart 2000–2005

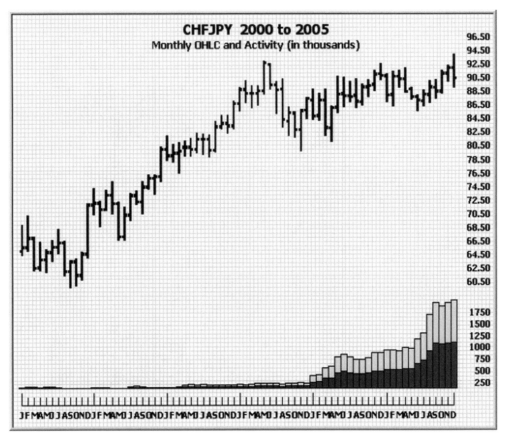

FIGURE 19.6 CHFJPY OHLC and Activity Chart 2000–2005

DAILY OHLC AND ACTIVITY CHARTS

This section uses the time frame 1/1/2006 to 4/14/2006 as the basis for daily OHLC and activity charts in the six cross rate currency pairs. (See Figures 19.7 through 19.12.)

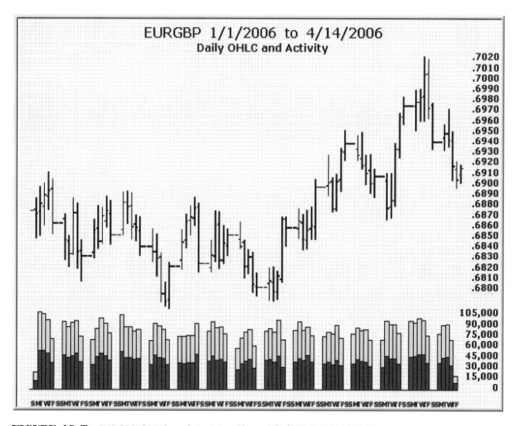

FIGURE 19.7 EURGBP OHLC and Activity Chart 1/1/2006–4/14/2006

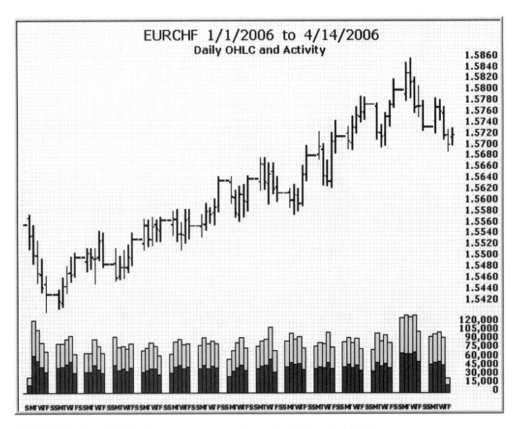

FIGURE 19.8   EURCHF OHLC and Activity Chart 1/1/2006–4/14/2006

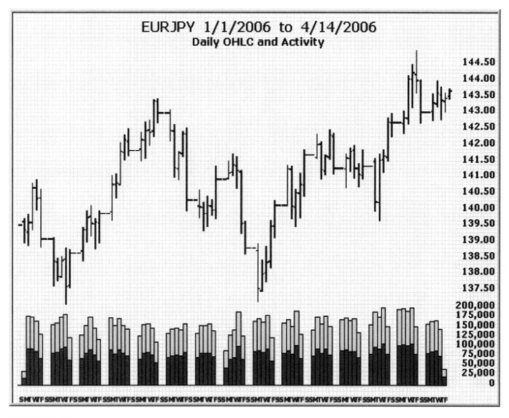

FIGURE 19.9   EURJPY OHLC and Activity Chart 1/1/2006–4/14/2006

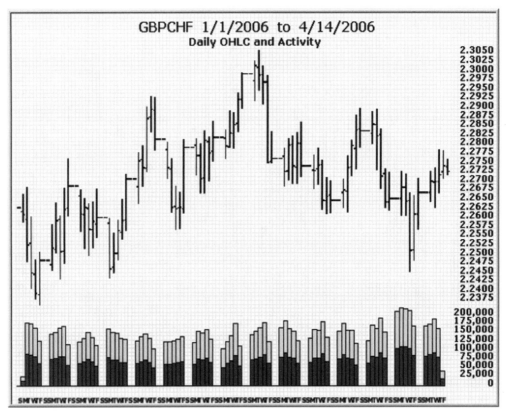

FIGURE 19.10   GBPCHF OHLC and Activity Chart 1/1/2006–4/14/2006

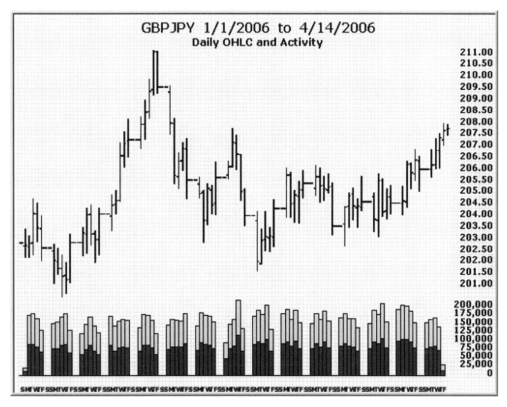

FIGURE 19.11 GBPJPY OHLC and Activity Chart 1/1/2006–4/14/2006

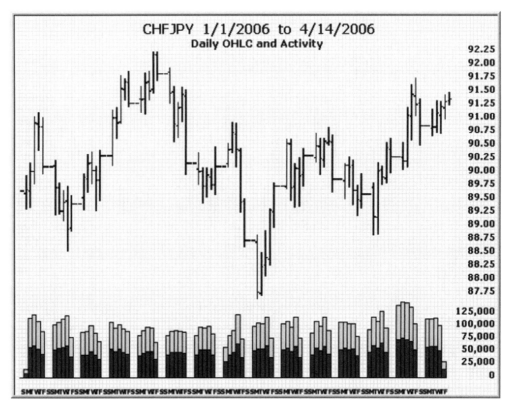

FIGURE 19.12   CHFJPY OHLC and Activity Chart 1/1/2006–4/14/2006

COMPOSITE ACTIVITY CHARTS

The composite charts in this section have a time frame spanning 1/1/2005 to 4/14/2006 daily composite activity charts for six cross rates. (See Figures 19.13 through 19.18.)

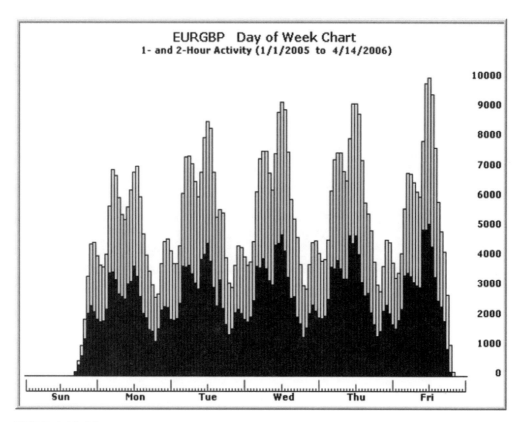

FIGURE 19.13 EURGBP Composite Activity Chart

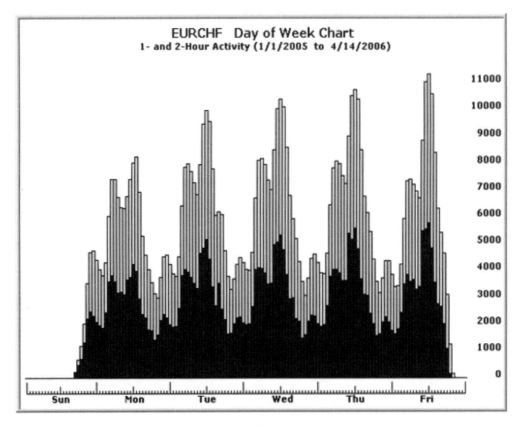

FIGURE 19.14 EURCHF Composite Activity Chart

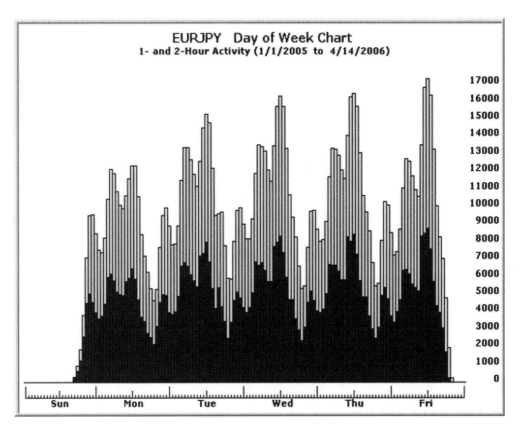

FIGURE 19.15 EURJPY Composite Activity Chart

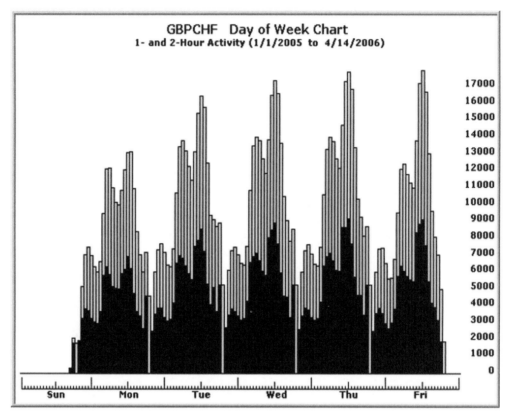

FIGURE 19.16 GBPCHF Composite Activity Chart

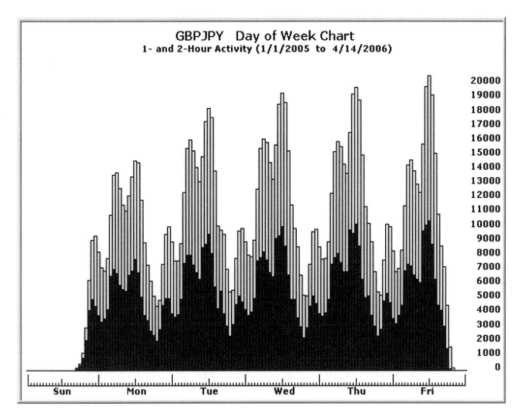

FIGURE 19.17 GBPJPY Composite Activity Chart

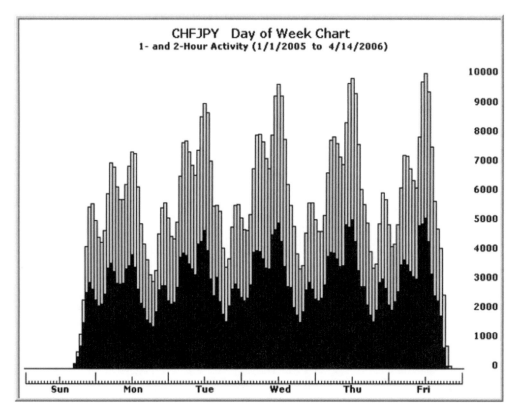

FIGURE 19.18   CHFJPY Composite Activity Chart

By convention, most currency data providers express date and time as U.S. Eastern Time (a format that we use throughout this book also). It is interesting to note how much the different cross rate composite charts vary due to the differences in global banking hours. See Appendix C for a table of global banking periods.

CHAPTER 20

Cross Rate Statistics

CROSS RATE ACTIVITY SUMMARY

Tables 20.1 and 20.2 show a comparison of activity between cross rates and USD major currencies for the time frame 1/1/2005 through 4/14/2006.

TABLE 20.1 Cross Rate Activity

Currency	Upticks	Downticks	Activity
EURGBP	318,197,106	317,236,750	635,433,856
EURCHF	369,830,595	379,228,858	749,059,453
EURJPY	591,791,530	609,238,793	1,201,030,323
GBPCHF	595,421,070	576,094,525	1,171,515,595
GBPJPY	674,085,176	674,717,234	1,348,802,410
CHFJPY	315,365,775	329,132,994	644,498,769

TABLE 20.2 USD Major Currency Activity

Currency	Upticks	Downticks	Activity
EURUSD	547,639,484	567,189,089	1,114,828,573
GBPUSD	594,607,675	627,664,473	1,222,272,148
USDCHF	552,015,832	582,785,614	1,134,801,446
USDJPY	469,593,946	516,389,523	985,983,469

SINGLE CURRENCY ACTIVITY

By arranging all five major currencies in a two-dimensional matrix format and adding each row, we can determine the total activity of each individual currency. In Table 20.3, values are expressed in millions of ticks.

This is somewhat of a surprising result. (See Table 20.4.) By virtue of the fact that the EMU is composed of twelve member nations and three of these are members of the Group of Eight (G8), we anticipated a much higher position for the Euro. G8 consists of the United States, UK, Japan, Germany, France, Italy, Canada, and the Russian Federation. They represent 67 percent of the world economy

Therefore we performed the same analysis on the same five currencies but with an earlier time frame spanning 1/1/2000 through 12/31/2003; this is shown in Table 20.5.

TABLE 20.3 Two-Dimensional Matrix Format

	EUR	GBP	USD	CHF	JPY	Total
EUR	—	635	1,115	749	1,201	3,700
GBP	635	—	1,222	1,172	1,349	4,378
USD	1,115	1,222	—	1,135	986	4,458
CHF	749	1,172	1,135	—	645	3,701
JPY	1,201	1,349	986	645	—	4,181

TABLE 20.4	Currencies Sorted by Activity Percentage
USD	21.83
GBP	21.44
JPY	20.48
CHF	18.13
EUR	18.12

TABLE 20.5	Currencies Sorted by Percentage (2000–2003)
USD	27.90
EUR	22.82
GBP	18.85
JPY	17.75
CHF	12.68

This confirms the rather obvious hypothesis that the currency markets are in perpetual flux (not just price, but volatility and activity also) and that indicators which may be valid at one time may not be valid at a later time. Also it is estimated that these five currencies comprise 78 percent of all trading in the foreign exchange markets.

Again we must reiterate that tick activity is not a direct substitute for volume and open interest but is nonetheless a valid statistic for volatility studies.

PART VII

Comparative Studies

CHAPTER 21

Major Currencies and Currency Futures

OVERVIEW

A futures contract is an agreement between two parties: A short position is taken by the party who agrees to deliver a commodity, and a long position is taken by the party who agrees to receive a commodity on a pre-arranged date. For example, a grain farmer would be the holder of the short position (agreeing to sell the grain), while the bakery would be the holder of the long position (agreeing to buy the grain).

In every futures contract, everything is precisely specified: the quantity and quality (or grade) of the underlying commodity, the specific price per unit, and the date and method of delivery. The price of a futures contract is represented by the agreed-upon price of the underlying commodity or financial instrument that will be delivered in the future. For example, in the above scenario, the size of the contract is 5,000 bushels of soft red #2 wheat at a price of 317 cents per bushel, and the delivery date may be the third Wednesday in September of the current year.

The Forex market is essentially a cash or spot market in which over 90 percent of the trades are liquidated within 48 hours. Currency trades held longer than this are normally routed through an authorized commodity futures exchange such as the International Monetary Market (IMM). It was founded in 1972 and is a division of the Chicago Mercantile Exchange (CME) that specializes in currency futures, interest-rate futures, and stock index futures, as well as options on futures. Clearing houses (the futures exchange) and introducing brokers are subject to more stringent regulations from the SEC, CFTC, and NFA agencies than the Forex spot market (see www.cme.com and www.cbot.com for more details).

FUTURES VOLUME AND OPEN INTEREST

Volume is the number of futures contracts traded within a given time period. Open interest is the number of open futures contracts at any given time. Even though the volume and open interest of Forex spot currencies are presently not accessible, it is still possible to compare them with currency futures just as a point of perspective. Table 21.1 summarizes the trading activity of selected futures contracts in currencies, precious metals, and some financial instruments. The volume and open interest readings are intended only to provide a brief synopsis of each market's liquidity and volatility based on the average of 30 trading days.

Table 21.2 lists the identical contracts but for the date June 4, 2004.

Note that all currency contracts (except the Canadian Dollar) exhibited a significant increase in volume and most showed an increase in open interest over the five-month time frame.

TABLE 21.1 Selected Futures Volume and Open Interest 1/16/2004

Market	Sym	Exch	Vol	OI
Eurodollar	ED	CME	93.9	772.5
Eurocurrency	EC	CME	49.5	112.9
10-yr. T-Note	TY	CBOT	43.1	676.4
Gold	GC	NYMEX	33.7	163.0
5-yr. T-Note	FV	CBOT	29.6	582.8
30-yr. T-Bond	US	CBOT	25.9	324.1
Japanese Yen	JY	CME	18.6	132.1
Canadian Dollar	CD	CME	18.0	64.2
British Pound	BP	CME	12.2	58.3
Silver	SI	NYMEX	10.0	84.2
Swiss Franc	SF	CME	9.3	45.6
Mexican Peso	ME	CME	8.8	30.5
Aussie Dollar	AD	CME	7.8	55.7
2-yr. T-Note	TU	CME	7.0	108.6
Copper	HG	NYMEX	4.2	32.8

Legend:
Sym: Ticker symbol.
Exch: Futures exchange on which contract is traded.
Vol: 30-day average daily volume, in thousands.
OI: Open interest, in thousands.

Source: Active Trader Magazine, Jan. 16, 2004 (www.activetradermag.com)

TABLE 21.2 Selected Futures Volume and Open Interest 6/4/2004

Market	Sym	Exch	Vol	OI
Eurodollar	ED	CME	152.8	844.9
Eurocurrency	EC	CME	66.1	132.6
10-year T-Note	TY	CBOT	67.7	1120.0
Gold	GC	NYMEX	44.8	125.1
5-year T-Note	FV	CBOT	46.0	935.7
30-year T-Bond	US	CBOT	29.3	451.7
Japanese Yen	JY	CME	21.6	106.9
Canadian Dollar	CD	CME	16.8	71.6
British Pound	BP	CME	14.0	45.5
Silver	SI	NYMEX	15.9	52.8
Swiss Franc	SF	CME	12.1	38.2
Mexican Peso	ME	CME	10.9	55.7
Aussie Dollar	AD	CME	8.2	35.5
2-year T-Note	TU	CME	8.8	176.2
Copper	HG	NYMEX	6.0	19.8

PIP DIFFERENTIAL OSCILLATOR

Figures 21.1 and 21.2 are the comparison charts for the EURUSD and the GBPUSD currency pairs. In both cases, the spot currency prices are displayed in the upper third of the chart. In the center is displayed the corresponding futures currency. In the lower section of the chart is displayed the Pip Differential Oscillator derived as follows:

$$\text{Pip Differential Oscillator} = 10{,}000 \times \text{Spot Close} - 10{,}000 \times \text{Futures Close}$$

First, the explanation of the Chicago Mercantile Exchange (CME) ticker symbols is:

$$\text{ECM4} = \text{Eurocurrency June 2004}$$
$$\text{BPM4} = \text{British Pound June 2004}$$

where June 2004 is the expiration (or delivery) month.

Our first observation is that the spot data has a greater daily range than the futures data, which we attribute to its greater trading activity. Also, futures contracts are usually thin markets during their infancy and grow more liquid as they mature, the result of increased volume and open interest.

Interesting to note is that, in Figure 21.1, the price differential oscillates on both sides of a zero mean while, in the second chart, the spot price is almost always higher than the futures price. This anomaly can probably be explained, though with

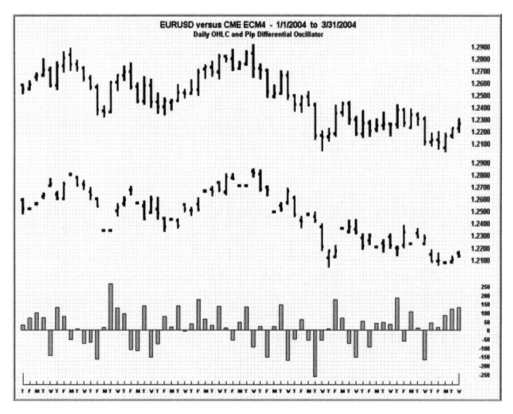

FIGURE 21.1 Pip Differential Oscillator—ECM4

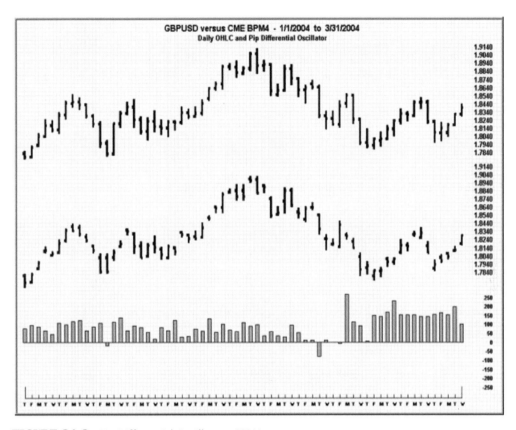

FIGURE 21.2 Pip Differential Oscillator—BPM4

some tedious research, by the changes in short term interest rates between the three currencies involved (USD, EUR, and GBP). Veteran commodity traders will probably recognize this phenomenon as a variation of "backwardization."

Also the fact that the pip differential oscillator for EURUSD/ECM4 does in fact undulate around a zero mean brings up an important point. There may be a very profitable leader/lagger relationship between the two financial vehicles if a discernible pattern can be uncovered.

ACTIVITY VERSUS VOLUME AND OPEN INTEREST

In Figures 21.3 and 21.4, the upper section displays the daily activity of the Forex currency pair. The volume and open interest of the currency futures contract are displayed in the middle and bottom sections respectively.

The above offers only a preliminary visual comparison between Forex activity and futures volume. Exhaustive studies between spot and futures currency prices may reveal a plethora of trading opportunities, particularly when anomalies occur.

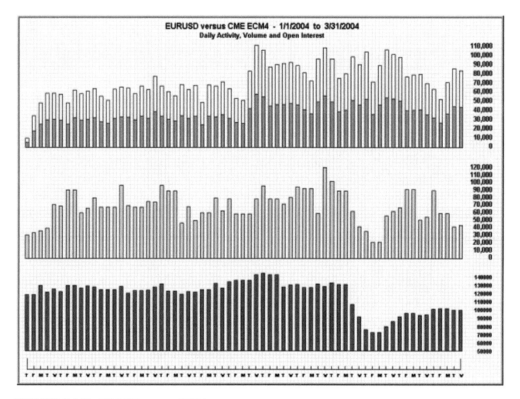

FIGURE 21.3　EURUSD versus ECM4

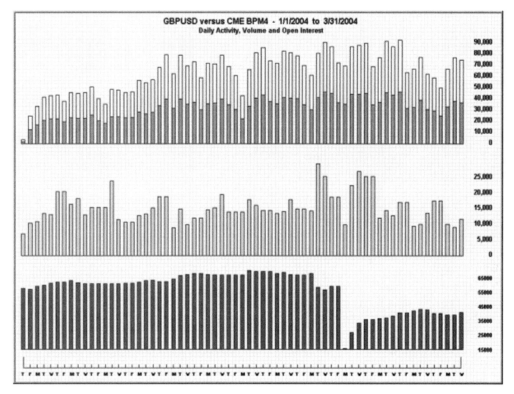

FIGURE 21.4   GBPUSD versus BPM4

CHAPTER 22

Major Currencies and Precious Metals

OVERVIEW

Universal fascination with gold is an obvious understatement. All Forex and futures traders are very intrigued about the correlation between precious metal prices and currency prices.

The ISO (International Standards Organization) designation for gold is XAU, where "X" is the identifier for financial vehicles other than currencies and "AU" is short for aurum, Latin for gold. Spot gold prices are represented in the same manner as Forex currency pairs: base currency on the left and quote currency on the right. XAU is always the base currency in the pair when quoting gold prices. Examples are XAUUSD, XAUEUR, XAUGBP, and XAUCHF.

Live spot gold prices are available through several gold dealers and news services such as those shown in Table 22.1.

TABLE 22.1 Major U.S. and British Spot Gold Dealers

Gold Information Network	www.goldinfo.net
Kitco	www.kitco.com
American Precious Metals Exchange	www.ampex.com
Gold Masters	www.goldmasters.com
Gold Prices	www.goldprices.com
London Metal Exchange	www.metalprices.com
Bullion Direct	www.bulliondirect.com

The streaming spot prices represent what gold customers are willing to pay at the current moment in time for gold coins, bullion, ingots, bars, wafers, and so on.

Historical data on compact disks for spot gold prices is available through Disk Trading, Ltd., and the quotes are supplied in the identical format as currency pairs. Thus upticks and downticks are supplied with time intervals of one minute and higher.

GOLD CHARTS

All Figures in this chapter use the same time frame from 1/1/2006 to 4/14/2006 with a constant time interval of one day. (See Figures 22.1 through 22.6.)

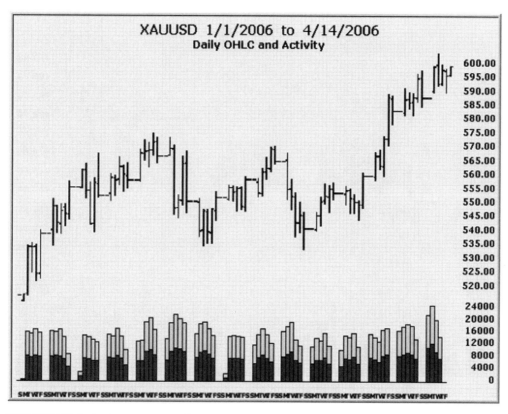

FIGURE 22.1   XAUUSD OHLC and Activity

XAUUSD Properties

Open	517.0200
High	604.3000
Low	515.0200
Close	599.8000
Mean	559.2728
Midrange	559.6600
Absolute Range	89.2800
Relative Range	15.9525
Standard Deviation	16.9720

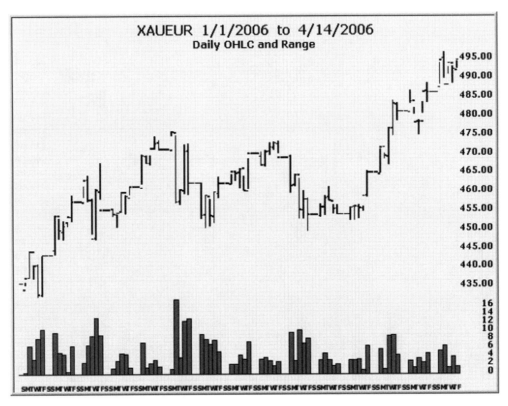

FIGURE 22.2   XAUEUR OHLC and Range

XAUEUR Properties

Open	436.3406
High	497.1208
Low	432.9051
Close	495.2523
Mean	464.1988
Midrange	465.0129
Absolute Range	64.2157
Relative Range	13.8094
Standard Deviation	12.8796

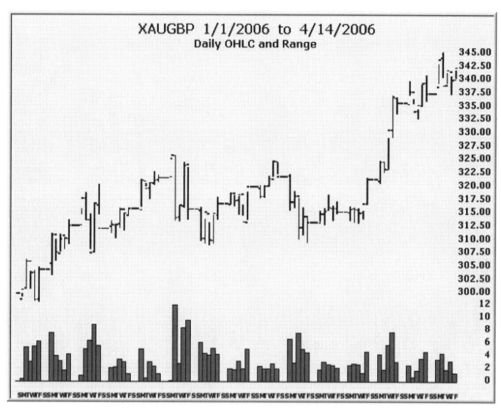

FIGURE 22.3   XAUGBP OHLC and Range

XAUGBP Properties

Open	300.0348
High	345.3932
Low	298.6238
Close	342.5667
Mean	319.1775
Midrange	322.0085
Absolute Range	46.7694
Relative Range	14.5243
Standard Deviation	9.8857

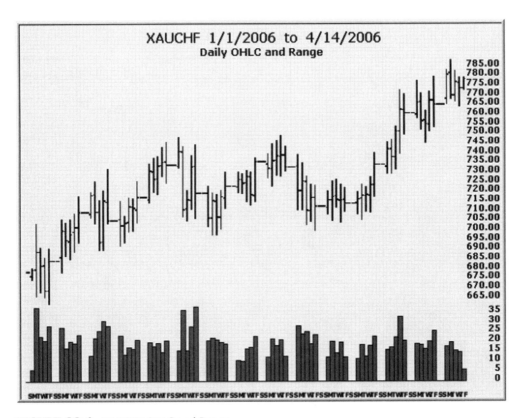

FIGURE 22.4 XAUCHF OHLC and Range

XAUCHF Properties

Open	679.1575
High	788.4906
Low	662.7868
Close	778.7803
Mean	725.0443
Midrange	725.6387
Absolute Range	125.7038
Relative Range	17.3232
Standard Deviation	23.6191

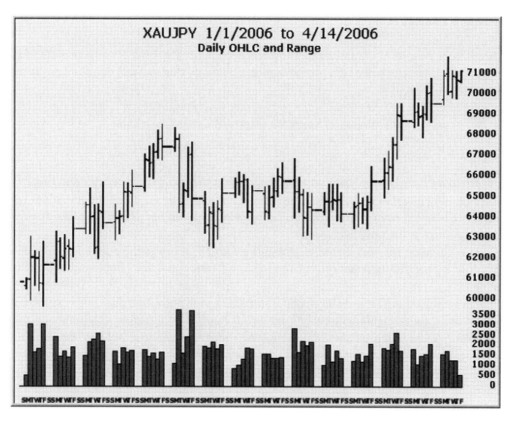

FIGURE 22.5 XAUJPY OHLC and Range

XAUJPY Properties

Open	60879.1050
High	71863.3560
Low	59731.3490
Close	71190.2620
Mean	65472.6052
Midrange	65797.3525
Absolute Range	12132.0070
Relative Range	18.4384
Standard Deviation	2351.3307

GOLD STATISTICS

There are a couple of statistical methods to determine just how closely an individual currency follows the price of a precious metal. The one that we will employ here is the coefficient of variation:

$$\text{Coefficient of Variation} = \frac{100 \times \text{Standard Deviation}}{\text{Mean}}$$

The reasoning behind this choice is based upon the fact that the coefficient of variation is a percentage or a dimensionless index number, while all the other statistical values given beneath each chart above are values expressed in terms of the quote currency (relative range is the only exception).

The rationale for correlation is straightforward: The lower the coefficient of variation, the higher the correlation between that currency and the precious metal. (See Table 22.2.)

These values are interesting from a statistical viewpoint but may not carry much weight as a forecasting indicator since numerous fundamental factors also influence gold and silver prices, such as production, mining, reserves, imports, exports, price-fixing, and so on.

TABLE 22.2 Major Currency Correlation with Gold

Currency	Coefficient of Variation
XAUEUR	2.77
XAUUSD	3.03
XAUGBP	3.10
XAUCHF	3.26
XAUJPY	3.59

SILVER CHARTS

The ISO designation for silver is XAG, from *argentum*, Latin for silver. The following analysis employs the same methodology and time frame as the gold study above. (See Figures 22.6 through 22.10.)

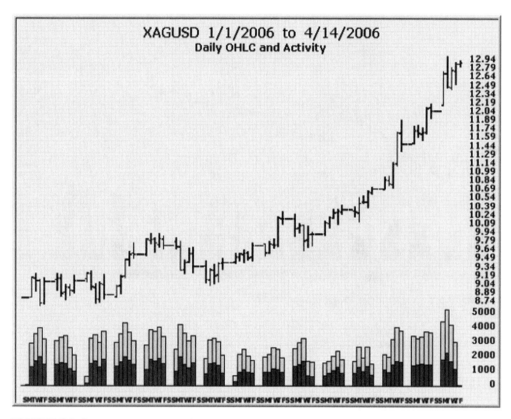

FIGURE 22.6 XAGUSD OHLC and Activity

XAGUSD Properties

Open	8.8250
High	13.0300
Low	8.6950
Close	12.9250
Mean	10.0411
Midrange	10.8625
Absolute Range	4.3350
Relative Range	39.9079
Standard Deviation	1.0431

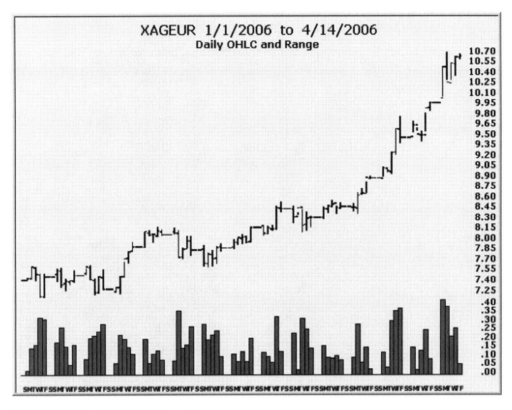

FIGURE 22.7 XAGEUR OHLC and Range

XAGEUR Properties

Open	7.4479
High	10.7190
Low	7.2068
Close	10.6721
Mean	8.3330
Midrange	8.9629
Absolute Range	3.5122
Relative Range	39.1859
Standard Deviation	0.8443

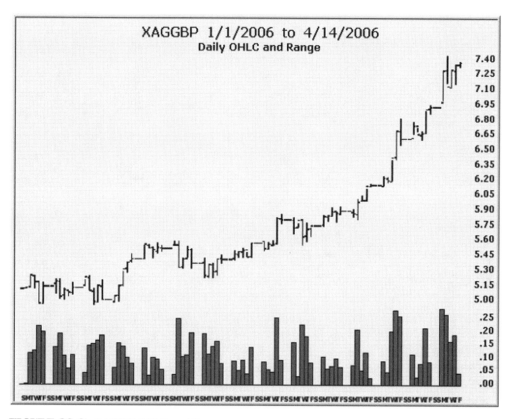

FIGURE 22.8 XAGGBP OHLC and Range

XAGGBP Properties

Open	5.1213
High	7.4474
Low	4.9673
Close	7.3819
Mean	5.7321
Midrange	6.2074
Absolute Range	2.4801
Relative Range	39.9544
Standard Deviation:	0.6122

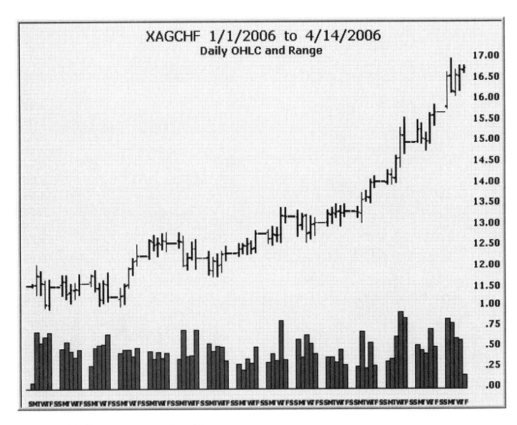

FIGURE 22.9   XAGCHF OHLC and Range

XAGCHF Properties

Open	11.5925
High	17.0015
Low	11.0454
Close	16.7818
Mean	13.0216
Midrange	14.0235
Absolute Range	5.9562
Relative Range	42.4728
Standard Deviation	1.4000

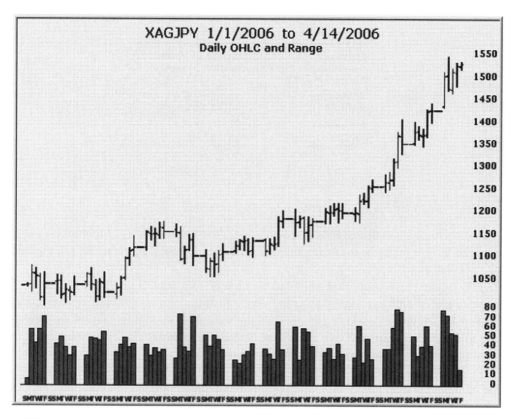

FIGURE 22.10 XAGJPY OHLC and Range

XAGJPY Properties

Open	1039.1438
High	1549.5276
Low	995.4273
Close	1534.0683
Mean	1176.0229
Midrange	1272.4775
Absolute Range	554.1003
Relative Range	43.5450
Standard Deviation	129.5541

TABLE 22.3 Major Currency Correlation with Silver

Currency	Coefficient of Variation
XAGEUR	10.13
XAGUSD	10.39
XAGGBP	10.63
XAGCHF	10.75
XAGJPY	11.02

SILVER STATISTICS

Analogous to the gold study above, we will again use the coefficient of variation as an indicator to determine how closely major currencies follow the prevailing price of silver. (See Table 22.3.)

It is interesting to note that after the coefficients of variation for both gold and silver were sorted with the highest correlation at the top, the major currencies are in the same order. However, none of the coefficients exhibited enough deviation or uniqueness to devise any hard and fast rules that traders can employ presently. We intend to probe this side venue of currency trading in more detail.

CAVEAT

Both trading in spot precious metals and currency trading have their intrinsic risk/reward factors. Readers should be aware of one interesting historical note on the volatility of silver prices.

In 1973 the Hunt family of Texas began taking delivery on silver futures contracts as a hedge against inflation when silver was in the $1.95 per ounce range. By 1979, the Hunt brothers (Nelson Bunker and William Herbert), with the assistance of some wealthy Arabs, amassed over 200 million ounces of silver, accounting for nearly half of the world's deliverable supply.

In early 1980, silver peaked at $54 per ounce, then plummeted on March 17 from $21.62 to $10.80 in a single day. A combination of changed trading rules on the New York Metals Market (COMEX) and the intervention of the Federal Reserve brought the entire fiasco to a close and in 1988 the Hunt brothers were convicted of conspiring to manipulate the market when their liabilities had grown to $2.5 billion against assets of $1.5 billion.

Amazingly, there is an upside to this rather scary tale. Numerous economists proclaim that market prices are merely the result of random walk theory and that technical analysis is simply human folly. The history of silver prices alone refutes this myopic claim, since the rise and collapse of silver prices in the 1970s and 1980s can be attributed directly to supply and demand, a fundamental influence directly related to technical analysis. Given the history of silver prices from 1789 to 1973 as a mathematical database, the likelihood of hitting a price of $54 in the subsequent seven years is not impossible using random walk theory, merely astronomically small. The moral is simple: Never initiate a currency trade without a stop loss limit order. Also, it is not wise to trade securities under SEC investigation regardless of how lucrative they may appear to be.

CHAPTER 23

The Mundo Currency

OVERVIEW

The *Mundo* is a pragmatic concoction of co-author Jim Bickford and represents a synthetic global spot currency. In some ways it is analogous to the U.S. Dollar Index (ticker symbol DX), which is an openly traded futures contract offered by the New York Board of Trade since 1973. The U.S. Dollar Index is computed using a trade-weighted geometric average of the forward futures contracts of the six currencies listed in Table 23.1.

IMM currency futures traders monitor the U.S. Dollar Index to gauge the dollar's overall performance in world currency markets. If the U.S. Dollar Index is trading lower, then it is very likely that a major currency that is a component of the Index is trading higher.

TABLE 23.1 U.S. Dollar Index Components	
Currency	**Weight %**
Euro Currency	57.6
Japanese Yen	13.6
British Pound	11.9
Canadian Dollar	9.1
Swedish Krona	4.2
Swiss Franc	1.6

INTERNATIONAL CURRENCY UNIT

Stock and commodity traders have numerous composite indices which can be used as barometers in the selection of which securities to trade. Outside of the U.S. Dollar Index, spot currency traders have none. For that purpose, we created the hypothetical currency, the International Currency Unit, and nicknamed it the *Mundo* for short. We will give it a fictitious ISO (International Standards Organization) designation of "ICU." The Mundo will be used to define the arithmetic average of a *selection* of spot currency pairs.

MUNDO CALCULATION

In this study of U.S. major currency pairs, we will restrict our selection of Mundo components to EURUSD, GBPUSD, USDCHF, and USDJPY.

The first step is to ensure that the USD is the quote currency in each pair, which means the arithmetic reciprocal must be substituted for the USDCHF and USDJPY pairs.

The second step is to convert all exchange rates to integral pip amounts. This means multiplying 10,000 times the exchange rates for the EURUSD, GBPUSD, and CHFUSD pairs. Multiply the JPYUSD by 100,000.

The final step is to sum the four pairs and divide by four. To convert the pips back to an exchange rate, divide by 10,000.

Because the Mundo is an aggregate currency, it is natural to think that anomalies in the individual component currency pairs would be smoothed over for the most part. Yet a closer examination of the Mundo chart shows that anomalies appear to be accentuated.

In Figure 23.1, note that the average activity is represented at the bottom.

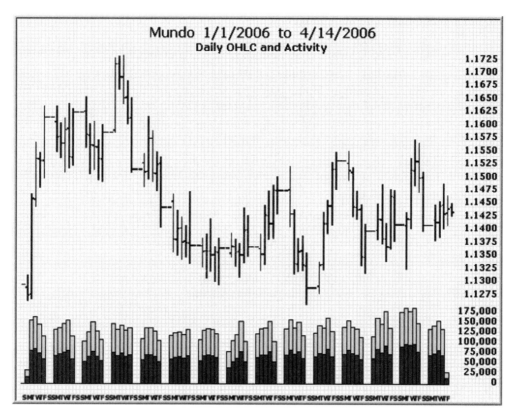

FIGURE 23.1 Mundo OHLC and Activity Chart

MUNDO DIFFERENTIAL CHART

The Mundo Differential Chart is a new addition to the technical analysis of spot currency pairs. Its purpose is to determine the degree of divergence that one USD major currency pair deviates from the Mundo currency comprised of the EURUSD, GBPUSD, CHFUSD, and JPYUSD pairs. (See Figures 23.2 through 23.5.)

In the upper portion of Figure 23.2 are two curves, one solid and one dotted. The solid line represents the daily closes in the EURUSD currency pair after the first close in the time series has been subtracted from all the subsequent closes. The same is true for the dotted line except that it represents the Mundo currency. This scaling operation coerces both time series to start at the same point on the left side of the chart.

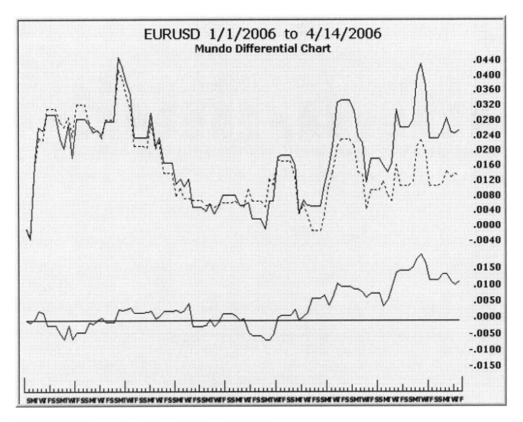

FIGURE 23.2   Mundo Differential Chart (EURUSD)

The solid curve in the lower portion of the chart is the difference between the two upper curves, that is, the scaled Mundo data is subtracted from the scaled EURUSD data.

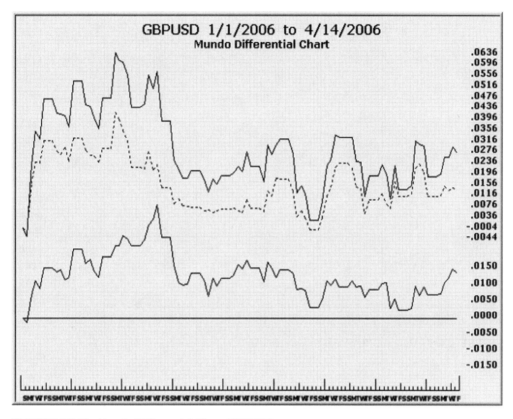

FIGURE 23.3 Mundo Differential Chart (GBPUSD)

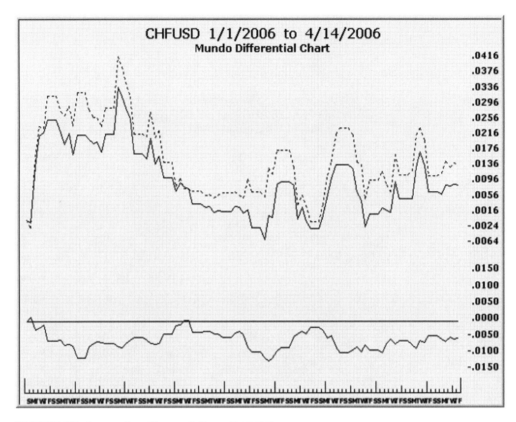

FIGURE 23.4 Mundo Differential Chart (CHFUSD)

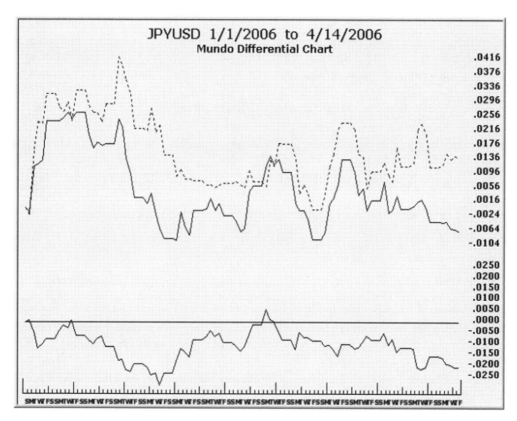

FIGURE 23.5   Mundo Differential Chart (JPYUSD)

The premise of the differential chart is based upon *transitivity*, the crucial element in arbitrage which relies on the equilibrium formula to keep all currency pairs in balance with each other. The simplest form of transitivity occurs in triangular arbitrage, which involves exactly three currencies:

$$EURUSD = EURGBP \times GBPUSD$$

An example of equilibrium involving all five major currencies is:

$$EURUSD = (EURGBP / GBPCHF) \times (CHFJPY/USDJPY)$$

Note that each single currency appears exactly twice in the formula above.

USAGE

The differential chart is experimental and still requires thorough testing. One observation is that when the scaled major currency pair exceeds an arbitrary number of pips above the scaled Mundo currency, an upward trend is indicated. The converse appears true for a downward trend also.

Leader/lagger relationships (also called dominance and dependence) may also be detected by the use of the Mundo differential chart. (See Figure 23.6.)

The authors are currently involved in writing online software that will test the deviation of a single currency pair from the Mundo as a potential market entry indicator. The difficulty is that, while arbitrage opportunities are frequently present, they are usually very short-lived.

Lastly, the authors wish to state that the readers should not restrict themselves to trades that involve only the major currencies. There are numerous trading opportunities with the minor currency pairs also (such as the Canadian Dollar, the Australian Dollar, the New Zealand Dollar, the Swedish Krona, the Hong Kong Dollar, the Singapore Dollar, and several others). In fact, many of these exhibit greater volatility than the major currency pairs. The disadvantage, though, is their diminished liquidity. So it is expedient to schedule trading sessions during periods of peak activity when dealing with the minor currency pairs.

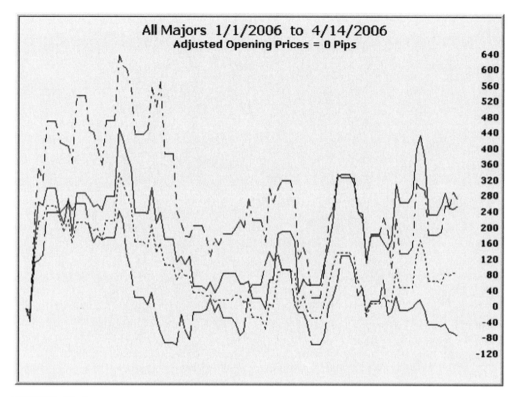

FIGURE 23.6 All Four USD Majors

Legend:

USD Major	Line Style	Close
GBPUSD	Dots and Dashes	275
EURUSD	Solid Line	248
CHFUSD	Dots Only	81
JPYUSD	Dashes Only	−82

Appendixes

ISO Currencies Pairs

This is a list of global currencies and the three-character currency codes that we have found are generally used to represent them. Often, but not always, this code is the same as the ISO 4217 standard. (The ISO, or International Organization for Standardization, is a worldwide federation of national standards.)

In most cases, the currency code is composed of the country's two-character internet country code plus an extra character to denote the currency unit. For example, the code for Canadian Dollars is simply Canada's two-character internet country code ("CA") plus a one-character currency designator ("D").

We have endeavored to list the codes that, in our experience, are actually in general industry use to represent the currencies. Currency names are given in the plural form. This list does not contain obsolete Euro-zone currencies.

TABLE A.1 World Currencies

Symbol	Region	Currency Name
AED	United Arab Emirates	Dirhams
AFA	Afghanistan	Afghanis
ALL	Albania	Leke
AMD	Armenia	Drams
ANG	Netherlands Antilles	Guilders
AOA	Angola	Kwanza
ARS	Argentina	Pesos
AUD	Australia	Dollars
AWG	Aruba	Guilders
AZM	Azerbaijan	Manats
BAM	Bosnia, Herzegovina	Convertible Marka
BBD	Barbados	Dollars
BDT	Bangladesh	Taka
BGN	Bulgaria	Leva
BHD	Bahrain	Dinars
BIF	Burundi	Francs
BMD	Bermuda	Dollars
BND	Brunei Darussalam	Dollars
BOB	Bolivia	Bolivianos
BRL	Brazil	Brazil Real
BSD	Bahamas	Dollars
BTN	Bhutan	Ngultrum
BWP	Botswana	Pulas
BYR	Belarus	Rubles
BZD	Belize	Dollars
CAD	Canada	Dollars
CDF	Congo/Kinshasa	Congolese Francs
CHF	Switzerland	Francs
CLP	Chile	Pesos
CNY	China	Renminbi
COP	Colombia	Pesos
CRC	Costa Rica	Colones
CUP	Cuba	Pesos
CVE	Cape Verde	Escudos
CYP	Cyprus	Pounds
CZK	Czech Republic	Koruny
DJF	Djibouti	Francs
DKK	Denmark	Kroner
DOP	Dominican Republic	Pesos
DZD	Algeria	Algeria Dinars
EEK	Estonia	Krooni
EGP	Egypt	Pounds
ERN	Eritrea	Nakfa
ETB	Ethiopia	Birr
EUR	Euro Member Countries	Euro
FJD	Fiji	Dollars

(continues)

TABLE A.1 *(Continued)*

Symbol	Region	Currency Name
FKP	Falkland Islands	Pounds
GBP	United Kingdom	Pounds
GEL	Georgia	Lari
GGP	Guernsey	Pounds
GHC	Ghana	Cedis
GIP	Gibraltar	Pounds
GMD	Gambia	Dalasi
GNF	Guinea	Francs
GTQ	Guatemala	Quetzales
GYD	Guyana	Dollars
HKD	Hong Kong	Dollars
HNL	Honduras	Lempiras
HRK	Croatia	Kuna
HTG	Haiti	Gourdes
HUF	Hungary	Forint
IDR	Indonesia	Rupiahs
ILS	Israel	New Shekels
IMP	Isle of Man	Pounds
INR	India	Rupees
IQD	Iraq	Dinars
IRR	Iran	Rials
ISK	Iceland	Kronur
JEP	Jersey	Pounds
JMD	Jamaica	Dollars
JOD	Jordan	Dinars
JPY	Japan	Yen
KES	Kenya	Shillings
KGS	Kyrgyzstan	Soms
KHR	Cambodia	Riels
KMF	Comoros	Francs
KPW	Korea (North)	Won
KRW	Korea (South)	Won
KWD	Kuwait	Dinars
KYD	Cayman Islands	Dollars
KZT	Kazakstan	Tenge
LAK	Laos	Kips
LBP	Lebanon	Pounds
LKR	Sri Lanka	Rupees
LRD	Liberia	Dollars
LSL	Lesotho	Maloti
LTL	Lithuania	Litai
LVL	Latvia	Lati
LYD	Libya	Dinars
MAD	Morocco	Dirhams
MDL	Moldova	Lei
MGA	Madagascar	Ariary

(continues)

TABLE A.1 *(Continued)*

Symbol	Region	Currency Name
MKD	Macedonia	Denars
MMK	Myanmar (Burma)	Kyats
MNT	Mongolia	Tugriks
MOP	Macau	Patacas
MRO	Mauritania	Ouguiyas
MTL	Malta	Liri
MUR	Mauritius	Rupees
MVR	Maldives	Rufiyaa
MWK	Malawi	Kwachas
MXN	Mexico	Pesos
MYR	Malaysia	Ringgits
MZM	Mozambique	Meticais
NAD	Namibia	Dollars
NGN	Nigeria	Nairas
NIO	Nicaragua	Gold Cordobas
NOK	Norway	Krone
NPR	Nepal	Nepal Rupees
NZD	New Zealand	Dollars
OMR	Oman	Rials
PAB	Panama	Balboa
PEN	Peru	Nuevos Soles
PGK	Papua New Guinea	Kina
PHP	Philippines	Pesos
PKR	Pakistan	Rupees
PLN	Poland	Zlotych
PYG	Paraguay	Guarani
QAR	Qatar	Rials
ROL	Romania	Lei
RUR	Russia	Rubles
RWF	Rwanda	Rwanda Francs
SAR	Saudi Arabia	Riyals
SBD	Solomon Islands	Dollars
SCR	Seychelles	Rupees
SDD	Sudan	Dinars
SEK	Sweden	Kronor
SGD	Singapore	Dollars
SHP	Saint Helena	Pounds
SIT	Slovenia	Tolars
SKK	Slovakia	Koruny
SLL	Sierra Leone	Leones
SOS	Somalia	Shillings
SPL	Seborga	Luigini
SRG	Suriname	Guilders
STD	São Tome, Principe	Dobras
SVC	El Salvador	Colones
SYP	Syria	Pounds

(continues)

TABLE A.1　(*Continued*)

Symbol	Region	Currency Name
SZL	Swaziland	Emalangeni
THB	Thailand	Baht
TJS	Tajikistan	Somoni
TMM	Turkmenistan	Manats
TND	Tunisia	Dinars
TOP	Tonga	Pa'anga
TRL	Turkey	Liras
TTD	Trinidad, Tobago	Dollars
TVD	Tuvalu	Tuvalu Dollars
TWD	Taiwan	New Dollars
TZS	Tanzania	Shillings
UAH	Ukraine	Hryvnia
UGX	Uganda	Shillings
USD	United States of America	Dollars
UYU	Uruguay	Pesos
UZS	Uzbekistan	Sums
VEB	Venezuela	Bolivares
VND	Viet Nam	Dong
VUV	Vanuatu	Vatu
WST	Samoa	Tala
YER	Yemen	Rials
YUM	Yugoslavia	New Dinars
ZAR	South Africa	Rand
ZMK	Zambia	Kwacha
ZWD	Zimbabwe	Zimbabwe Dollars

Exchange Rates

The following table shows the international foreign exchange rates on 4/21/2006 compared with the USD.

TABLE B.1 Exchange Rates

Currency	Units/USD	USD/Units
Algerian Dinar	0.01379	72.52500
Argentine Peso	0.32701	3.05800
Australian Dollar	0.74420	1.34373
Baharaini Dinar	2.65266	0.37698
Bolivian Boliviano	0.12508	7.99500
Brazilian Real	0.47279	2.11510
British Pound	1.78280	0.56092
Botswana Pula	0.18714	5.34360
Canadian Dollar	0.87827	1.13860
Chilean Peso	0.00193	517.54999
Chinese Yuan	0.12477	8.01450
Columbian Peso	0.00043	2,337.00004
Cypriot Pound	2.14777	0.46560
Czech Koruna	0.04359	22.94200
Danish Krone	0.16547	6.04350
Ecuador Sucre	0.00004	25,000.00063
Euro	1.23450	0.81005
Ghanaian Cedi	0.00011	9,106.99988
Guatemalan Quetzal	0.13201	7.57500
Hong Kong Dollar	0.12897	7.75400
		(continues)

TABLE B.1 *(Continued)*

Currency	Units/USD	USD/Units
Hungarian Forint	0.00467	213.96001
Israeli Shekel	0.22015	4.54230
Indian Rupee	0.02216	45.13500
Indonesian Rupiah	0.00011	8,882.99974
Japanese Yen	0.00855	116.93001
Jordanian Dinar	1.41143	0.70850
Kenyan Shilling	0.01404	71.22000
Kuwaiti Dinar	3.42407	0.29205
Malaysian Ringgit	0.27319	3.66050
Mexican Peso	0.09016	11.09120
Moroccan Dirham	0.11191	8.93550
Namibian Dollar	0.16587	6.02900
New Zealand Dollar	0.63330	1.57903
Norwegian Krone	0.15748	6.35000
Omani Rial	2.59774	0.38495
Pakistan Rupee	0.01668	59.97000
Peruvian Nuevo Sol	0.30233	3.30770
Qatari Rial	0.27467	3.64070
Russian Rouble	0.03639	27.48000
Saudi Riyal	0.26663	3.75050
Singapore Dollar	0.62661	1.59590
South African Rand	0.16707	5.98550
South Korean Won	0.00106	948.00005
Swedish Krona	0.13248	7.54860
Swiss Franc	0.78475	1.27430
Taiwan Dollar	0.03098	32.27500
Algerian Dinar	0.01379	72.52500
Tanzanian Shilling	0.00083	1,211.99996
Thai Baht	0.02645	37.81000
Tunisian Dinar	0.74738	1.33800
Turkish Lira	0.75683	1.32130
UAR Emirati Dirham	0.27228	3.67270
US Dollar	1.00000	1.00000
Venezualan Bolivar	0.00047	2,144.00005
Vietnamese Dong	0.00006	15,924.99916
Zimbabwe Dollar	0.00001	99,202.00100

It is interesting to note that as of 4/21/2006 only six world currencies have a parity rate with the USD greater than 1.0000: Kuwaiti Dinar (3.42407), Baharaini Dinar (2.65266), Omani Rial (2.59774), Cypriot Pound (2.14777), British Pound (1.78280), and the Euro (1.23450). Coincidentally, at the bottom of the list, both alphabetically and parity-wise, is the Zimbabwe Dollar, which requires over 99,000 to equal one USD.

Additional information on current exchange rates can be found at http://money central.msn.com/investor/market/rates.asp.

Global Banking Hours

Price fluctuations in the spot currency markets are essentially news-driven. Or more accurately, it is the human reaction to news-driven events that makes trading possible and profitable. How traders interpret these news events determines in which direction the market will travel. As in all financial markets, the foreign exchange also has its share of contrarians who keep runaway breakouts in check while supplying additional volatility to the overall situation.

Despite all the fundamental and technical influences on the foreign exchange, one major constant in determining periods of high volatility is the hours of operation for the central banks of each major currency country.

The following table emphasizes the importance of the effect of time of day on Forex market activity and volatility based on hours of operation around the globe. Because banking hours vary from country to country, we have arbitrarily set hours of operation from 9:00 A.M. to 5:00 P.M. for consistency. The top row is expressed as Central European Time (Greenwich Mean Time + 1 hour), which aligns with the Central Bank of Europe in Frankfurt, the most prestigious central bank in the European Monetary Union.

The table allows traders to view overlapping time periods when central banks for different currencies are operating and thus guarantee a certain degree of mutual activity.

For example, when banks open in New York City at 9:00 A.M. EST, the Frankfurt bank has already been operating for six hours. So there is a two-hour overlap of trading in the EURUSD currency pair on both sides of the Atlantic Ocean (9:00 A.M. to 11:00 A.M. EST). This can be readily recognized in the Time of Day Activity Chart for the EURUSD pair.

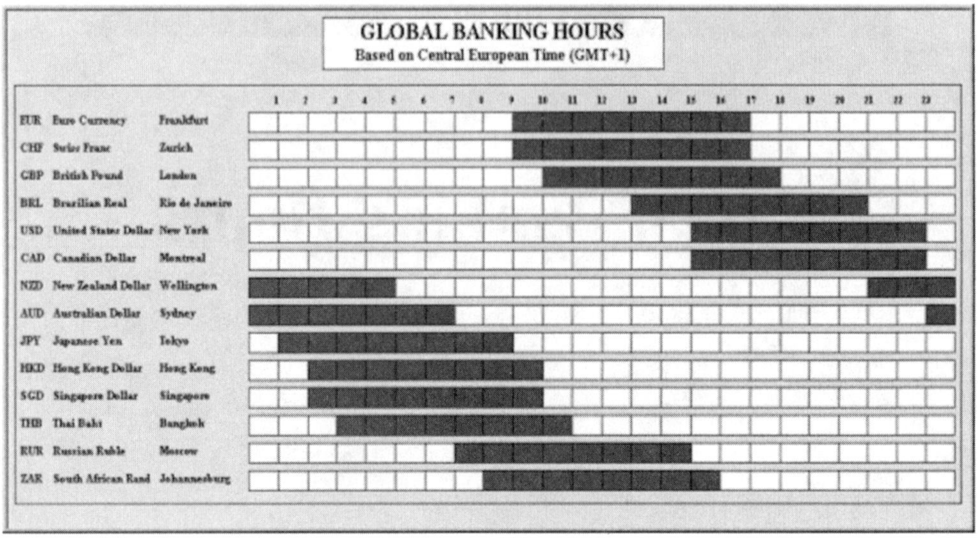

FIGURE C.1 Global Banking Hours

If we are interested in initiating a trade in the EURHKD cross rate pair, we note that there is a one-hour overlap in banking operations between central Europe and Hong Kong which occurs between 9:00 A.M. and 10:00 A.M. in Frankfurt (or 3:00 A.M. to 4:00 A.M. in New York).

Dedicated currency traders may have to adjust their sleeping schedules to take advantage of increased activity and volatility when trading non-USD cross rate currency pairs.

Internet

The amount of information now on the Internet about currency trading is enormous—a Google search finds over 2.2 million entries for "Forex"; inclusion herein does not represent an endorsement of any kind. We suggest beginning with one of the major portals such as www.goforex.net.

Online Brokers and Dealers

http://www.abwatley.com/forex/
http://www.ac-markets.com/
http://www.admisi.com
http://www.advancedfinancialworldwideinc.com
http://www.akmos.com/

http://www.alphaonetrading.com

http://www.ancofutures.com

http://www.apexforex.com

http://www.alipes.net

http://www.arcadiavest.com

http://www.axistrader.com

http://www.cbfx.com

http://www.charterfx.com/

http://www.choicefx.com/

http://www.cmc-forex.com

http://www.cms-forex.com/

http://www.coesfx.com

http://www.csfb.com

http://www.currencyconnect.net/

http://www.currencytradingusa.com

http://www.currencyuk.co.uk/

http://www.currenex.com

http://www.cytradefutures.com

http://www.dfgforex.com

http://www.directfx.com

http://www.dukascopy.com

http://www.eminilocal.com

http://www.enetspeculation.com/pub/en/defaut.asp

http://www.etradeprofessional.co.uk

http://www.fibo-forex.it

http://www.finanza.saav.biz

http://www.FlashForex.com

http://www.forex.com/

http://www.forex.ukrsotsbank.com

http://www.forexcapital.com/

http://www.forex-arabia.com

http://www.forex-day-trading.com/

http://www.forexforyou.com

http://www.forex-mg.com/

http://www.forex-millenium.com

http://www.forexsolutions.com/

http://www.forextradingusa.com

http://www.forextradingdirect.com

http://www.forexsystembroker.com/

http://www.fxadvantage.com/

http://www.fxall.com

http://www.fxcm.com/

http://www.fxdd.com

http://www.fxonline.co.jp

http://www.fxpremier.com/

http://www.fxsol.com/

http://www.fxtrader.net

http://www.fxtrading.com

http://www.gaincapital.com

http://www.gcitrading.com

http://www.gfsbroker.com

http://www.gftforex.com/

http://www.ggmk.com

http://www.gnitouch.com/

http://www.goldbergforex.com

http://www.guardianfx.com/

http://www.hawaii4x.com/

http://www.hotspotfx.com

http://www.ifxmarkets.com

http://www.interactivebrokers.com

http://www.interbankfx.com

http://www.invest2forex.com

http://www.kshitij.com/

http://www.mvpglobalforex.com

http://www.oio.com

http://www.pfgbest.com

http://www.powerforex.com

http://www.proedgefx.com

http://www.propfx.com

http://www.rcgtrader.com

http://www.realtimeforex.com

http://www.realtrade.lv

http://www.refcofx.com/

http://www.rjobrien.com

http://www.saxobank.com/

http://www.socofinance.com

http://www.sncinvestment.com

http://www.spencerfx.com

http://www.strategybroker.com

http://www.strikefx.com

http://www.superfutures.com

http://www.swissnetbroker.com

http://www.synthesisbank.com

http://www.titanfingroup.com

http://www.tradeamerican.com

http://www.tradestation.com

http://www.x-trade.biz

http://www.zaner.com

Data

http://www.ozforex.tradesecuring.com/misc/ozchart.asp

http://www.csidata.com

http://www.forexcapital.com/database.htm

http://www.olsendata.com/

http://www.disktrading.is99.com/disktrading/

http://www.cqg.com/products/datafactory.cfm

http://www.datastream.com/

http://www.tenfore.com/

http://www.dukascopy.com

http://www.netdania.com

http://www.pctrader.com

http://www.csidata.com

http://www.ebs.com/products/market-data.asp

http://www.infotecnet.com/

http://www.comstock-interactivedata.com/index.shtml

Charts

http://www.fxtrek.com

http://www.esignal.com

http://www.forex-markets.com/

http://www.forexcharts.com/

http://www.moneytec.com

http://www.global-view.com/beta/

http://www.fxstreet.com/

http://www.forexdirectory.net/

http://www.forex-markets.com/

Portals, Link Pages, and Forums

http://www.forexmagazine.com

http://www.moneytec.com

http://www.goforex.com

http://www.forexsites.com/

http://www.investorsresource.info/

http://www.global-view.com/beta/

http://www.fxstreet.com/

http://www.forexdirectory.net/

http://www.forexvision.com/

http://www.currencypro.com

http://www.forexcentral.net/

http://www.forexpoint.com/

http://www.piptrader.com/

http://www.forex-registry.com/

Software Development

http://www.snapdragon.co.uk/

http://www.fxpraxis.com

Performance Evaluation

http://www.parkerglobal.com/
http://www.marhedge.com/
http://www.barclaygrp.com/

Professional and Regulatory

http://www.aima.org/
http://www.cftc.gov/
http://www.nfa.futures.org/
http://www.mfainfo.org/
http://www.fiafii.org/

Co-Author Archer's Forex web site

http://www.fxpraxis.com

Resources

PERIODICALS

Active Trader (TechInfo, Inc.)—www.activetradermag.com

Futures (Futures Magazine, Inc.)—www.futuresmag.com

Currency Trader—www.currencytradermag.com

eForex—www.eforex.net

Euromoney—www.euromoney.com

Forex Magazine—www.forexmagazine.com

FX&MM—www.russellpublishing.com/FX&MM/index.html

FX Week—www.fxweek.com

GoForex—www.goforex.net

Technical Analysis of Stocks & Commodities—www.traders.com

Traders Journal—www.traders-journal.com

BOOKS

Aby, Carroll D., Jr. 1996. *Point & Figure Charting.* Greenville, SC: Traders Press.

Archer, Michael, and James Bickford. 2004. *Getting Started in Currency Trading.* Hoboken, NJ: Wiley.

Bickford, James. 2002. *Chart Plotting Techniques For Technical Analysts.* Boulder, CO: Syzygy.

Bigalow, Stephen. 2002. *Profitable Candlestick Trading.* Hoboken, NJ: Wiley.

Bulkowski, Thomas. 2005. *Encyclopedia of Chart Patterns.* Hoboken, NJ: Wiley.

Dorsey, Thomas. 1995. *Point & Figure Charting.* Hoboken, NJ: Wiley.

DraKoln, Noble. 2004. *Forex for Small Speculators.* Long Beach, CA: Enlightened Financial Press.

Henderson, Callum. 2002. *Currency Strategy.* Hoboken, NJ: Wiley.

Horner, Raghee. 2005. *Forex Trading for Maximum Profit.* Hoboken, NJ: Wiley.

Klopfenstein, Gary. 1993. *Trading Currency Cross Rates.* Hoboken, NJ: Wiley.

Lien, Kathy. 2004. *Day Trading the Currency Market.* Hoboken, NJ: Wiley.

Luca, Cornelius. 2000. *Technical Analysis Applications in the Global Currency Markets.* Upper Saddle River, NJ: Prentice Hall.

———. 2000. *Trading in the Global Currency Markets.* Upper Saddle River, NJ: Prentice Hall.

McGee, John. 2001. *Technical Analysis of Stock Trends.* New York: American Management Association.

Murphy, John. 2000. *Intermarket Financial Analysis.* Hoboken, NJ: Wiley.

———. 1999. *Technical Analysis of the Financial Markets.* Upper Saddle River, NJ: Prentice Hall.

Rosenstreich, Peter. 2004. *Forex Revolution.* Upper Saddle River, NJ: Prentice Hall.

Ross, Joe. 2001. *Trading by the Minute.* Cedar Park, TX: Joe Ross.

Schlossberg, Boris. 2006. *Technical Analysis of the Currency Market.* Hoboken, NJ: Wiley.

Shamah, Shani. 2003. *A Foreign Exchange Primer.* Hoboken, NJ: Wiley.

Zieg, Kermit. 1997. *Point & Figure.* Traders Press.

The world's largest supplier for mail-order trading books is Traders Press (http://www.traderspress.com).

INTERNET

The amount of information now on the Internet about currency trading is enormous—a Google search finds over 2.2 million entries for "Forex"; inclusion herein does not represent an endorsement of any kind. We suggest beginning with one of the major portals such as www.goforex.net.

ONLINE BROKERS AND DEALERS

http://www.abwatley.com/forex/

http://www.ac-markets.com/

http://www.admisi.com

http://www.advancedfinancialworldwideinc.com

http://www.akmos.com/

http://www.alphaonetrading.com

http://www.ancofutures.com

http://www.apexforex.com

http://www.alipes.net

http://www.arcadiavest.com

http://www.axistrader.com

http://www.cbfx.com

http://www.charterfx.com/

http://www.choicefx.com/

http://www.cmc-forex.com

http://www.cms-forex.com/

http://www.coesfx.com

http://www.csfb.com

http://www.currencyconnect.net/

http://www.currencytradingusa.com

http://www.currencyuk.co.uk/

http://www.currenex.com

http://www.cytradefutures.com

http://www.dfgforex.com

http://www.directfx.com

http://www.dukascopy.com

http://www.eminilocal.com

http://www.enetspeculation.com/pub/en/defaut.asp

http://www.etradeprofessional.co.uk

http://www.fibo-forex.it

http://www.finanza.saav.biz

http://www.FlashForex.com

http://www.forex.com/

http://www.forex.ukrsotsbank.com

http://www.forexcapital.com/

http://www.forex-arabia.com

http://www.forex-day-trading.com/

http://www.forexforyou.com

http://www.forex-mg.com/

http://www.forex-millenium.com

http://www.forexsolutions.com/

http://www.forextradingusa.com

http://www.forextradingdirect.com

http://www.forexsystembroker.com/

http://www.fxadvantage.com/

http://www.fxall.com

http://www.fxcm.com/

http://www.fxdd.com

http://www.fxonline.co.jp

http://www.fxpremier.com/

http://www.fxsol.com/

http://www.fxtrader.net

http://www.fxtrading.com

http://www.gaincapital.com

http://www.gcitrading.com

http://www.gfsbroker.com

http://www.gftforex.com/

http://www.ggmk.com

http://www.gnitouch.com/

http://www.goldbergforex.com

http://www.guardianfx.com/

http://www.hawaii4x.com/

http://www.hotspotfx.com

http://www.ifxmarkets.com

http://www.interactivebrokers.com

http://www.interbankfx.com

http://www.invest2forex.com

http://www.kshitij.com/

http://www.mvpglobalforex.com

http://www.oio.com

http://www.pfgbest.com

http://www.powerforex.com

http://www.proedgefx.com

http://www.propfx.com

http://www.rcgtrader.com

http://www.realtimeforex.com

http://www.realtrade.lv

http://www.refcofx.com/

http://www.rjobrien.com

http://www.saxobank.com/

http://www.socofinance.com

http://www.sncinvestment.com

http://www.spencerfx.com

http://www.strategybroker.com

http://www.strikefx.com

http://www.superfutures.com

http://www.swissnetbroker.com

http://www.synthesisbank.com

http://www.titanfingroup.com

http://www.tradeamerican.com

http://www.tradestation.com

http://www.x-trade.biz

http://www.zaner.com

DATA

http://www.ozforex.tradesecuring.com/misc/ozchart.asp

http://www.csidata.com

http://www.forexcapital.com/database.htm

http://www.olsendata.com/

http://www.disktrading.is99.com/disktrading/

http://www.cqg.com/products/datafactory.cfm

http://www.datastream.com/

http://www.tenfore.com/

http://www.dukascopy.com

http://www.netdania.com

http://www.pctrader.com

http://www.csidata.com

http://www.ebs.com/products/market-data.asp

http://www.infotecnet.com/

http://www.comstock-interactivedata.com/index.shtml

CHARTS

http://www.fxtrek.com

http://www.esignal.com

http://www.forex-markets.com/

http://www.forexcharts.com/

http://www.moneytec.com

http://www.global-view.com/beta/

http://www.fxstreet.com/

http://www.forexdirectory.net/

http://www.forex-markets.com/

PORTALS, LINK PAGES, AND FORUMS

http://www.forexmagazine.com

http://www.moneytec.com

http://www.goforex.com

http://www.forexsites.com/

http://www.investorsresource.info/

http://www.global-view.com/beta/

http://www.fxstreet.com/

http://www.forexdirectory.net/

http://www.forexvision.com/

http://www.currencypro.com

http://www.forexcentral.net/

http://www.forexpoint.com/

http://www.piptrader.com/

http://www.forex-registry.com/

SOFTWARE DEVELOPMENT

http://www.snapdragon.co.uk/

http://www.fxpraxis.com

PERFORMANCE EVALUATION

http://www.parkerglobal.com/
http://www.marhedge.com/
http://www.barclaygrp.com/

PROFESSIONAL AND REGULATORY

http://www.aima.org/
http://www.cftc.gov/
http://www.nfa.futures.org/
http://www.mfainfo.org/
http://www.fiafii.org/

CO-AUTHOR ARCHER'S FOREX WEB SITE

http://www.fxpraxis.com

Index